D1194014

WITHDRAWN

Connecticut Yankees at Gettysburg

# Connecticut

# Yankees at

# GETTYSBURG

by

Charles P. Hamblen

edited by

Walter L. Powell

The Kent State

University Press

Kent, Ohio,

and London, England

© 1993 by The Kent State University Press
Kent, Ohio 44242
ALL RIGHTS RESERVED
Library of Congress Catalog Card Number 92-34747
ISBN 0-87338-477-6 (cloth)
ISBN 0-87338-478-4 (pbk.)
Manufactured in the United States of America

03 02 01 00 99 98 97 96 95 94      6 5 4 3 2

Library of Congress Cataloging-in-Publication Data
Hamblen, Charles P., 1916–1986.
Connecticut Yankees at Gettysburg / by Charles P. Hamblen ; edited
by Walter L. Powell.
p.  cm.
Includes bibliographical references and index.
ISBN 0-87338-477-6 (cloth : alk. paper) ∞
ISBN 0-87338-478-4 (pbk. : alk. paper) ∞
1. Gettysburg (Pa.), Battle of, 1863.   2. Connecticut—History—Civil War,
1861–1865—Regimental histories.   3. United States—History—Civil War,
1861–1865—Regimental histories.
I. Powell, Walter Louis.   II. Title.
E475.53.H22   1993
973.7'349—dc20                    92-34747

British Library Cataloging-in-Publication data are available.

# CONTENTS

# LIST OF MAPS

# ACKNOWLEDGMENT

My family and I wish to acknowledge, with deep appreciation, the invaluable help and support of Dr. Walter L. Powell who, after the death of my husband, offered to assume the gigantic task of preparing the manuscript for publication.

For the many months of arduous editorial work involving compiling the bibliography and providing the additional materials and revision necessary for the manuscript's completion, we sincerely thank Dr. Powell, without whom my sons and I might not have experienced the great joy and satisfaction of seeing this book in print.

ELSIE M. HAMBLEN

# PREFACE

As with the events of the Battle of Gettysburg, fate sometimes takes a strange turn, and so it was with my first meeting with the author of this study, Charles Hamblen. In the fall of 1984 I had just submitted a proposal to the Connecticut Historical Society to do a slide lecture called "Connecticut at Gettysburg"; Charles sent a query to the Society at the same time requesting more information on their Civil War holdings. We met in Gettysburg in October, and I learned he had nearly completed the first draft of this study. During the next year we enjoyed a growing friendship, one developed through occasional meetings and a lively correspondence. I was deeply saddened by his untimely death in May 1986 and was pleased to offer my help to his family to see this work reach fruition.

On behalf of Mrs. Elsie Hamblen and her family, I would like to thank the following people and institutions whose assistance has made this work possible to complete: Michael Winey and Randy Hackenberg of the Photographic Division, United States Military History Institute, Carlisle Barracks, Pennsylvania; Elwood Christ, Gettysburg; William A. Frassanito, Gettysburg; W. E. Jordan, Gettysburg; Bob Prosperi and Kathy Georg Harrison, Gettysburg National Military Park; Edward Marcus and the staff of the New Canaan Historical Society, New Canaan, Connecticut; Paul Smith, McKnightstown, Pennsylvania; Karl Sundstrom, North Riverside, Illinois; Lewis Leigh, Fairfax, Virginia; Tom Riemor, Bristol, Connecticut; Walter Lane, The Lane Studio,

Gettysburg; the staffs of the Connecticut Historical Society and the Connecticut State Library, Hartford; the staffs of the Beinecke Rare Book and Manuscript Library and the Sterling Library, Yale University; and Mary Witkowski of the Bridgeport Public Library, Bridgeport, Connecticut. A very special thanks goes to my good friend Andy DeCusati, a dedicated Civil War buff and member of the reactivated 27th Connecticut Volunteers, who donated his time cheerfully to pursue research leads for me in New Haven and Bridgeport. Finally, but not least of all, I wish to thank my wife, Susan, whose patience and understanding has enabled me to steal a few hours from our children, Nat and Sally, to finish this book.

WALTER L. POWELL
Gettysburg

Connecticut Yankees at Gettysburg

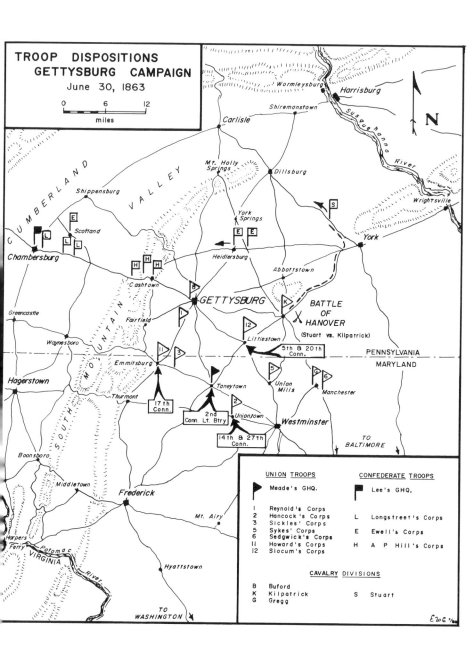

**TROOP DISPOSITIONS**
**GETTYSBURG CAMPAIGN**
June 30, 1863

0    6    12
miles

N

Wormleysburg    Harrisburg

Shiremanstown

Susquehanna River

Carlisle

Mt. Holly Springs    Dillsburg

CUMBERLAND    VALLEY

Shippensburg    Wrightsville

York Springs

E    Scotland    York

L    L    L    Heidlersburg    S

Chambersburg    Abbottstown

H    H    H

Cashtown    B    GETTYSBURG    K    BATTLE OF HANOVER

Greencastle    Fairfield    (Stuart vs. Kilpatrick)

Waynesboro    12    Littlestown    PENNSYLVANIA

11    3    5th & 20th Conn.    MARYLAND

Hagerstown    Emmitsburg    Taneytown    5    6    6

Union Mills    Manchester

Thurmont    17th Conn.    2    Uniontown    Westminster

2nd Conn. Lt. Btry.    14th & 27th Conn.    TO BALTIMORE

Boonsboro

Middletown    Frederick

Harpers Ferry    Mt. Airy

VIRGINIA    Potomac River

Hyattstown

TO WASHINGTON

| UNION TROOPS | | CONFEDERATE TROOPS |
|---|---|---|
| | Meade's GHQ. | Lee's GHQ. |
| 1 | Reynold's Corps | |
| 2 | Hancock's Corps | |
| 3 | Sickles' Corps | L  Longstreet's Corps |
| 5 | Sykes' Corps | |
| 6 | Sedgwick's Corps | E  Ewell's Corps |
| 11 | Howard's Corps | |
| 12 | Slocum's Corps | H  A P Hill's Corps |

CAVALRY DIVISIONS

B    Buford
K    Kilpatrick    S    Stuart
G    Gregg

# Connecticut on the March  **1**  The Roads to Gettysburg

There it happened. There is the way of the land.
There was the fate, and there the blind swords were
crossed.
                    —Stephen Vincent Benét, *John Brown's Body*

FROM WILMINGTON, DELAWARE, young Lt. William T. Lusk, a native of Norwich, Connecticut, dashed off these lines to his "Dear, dear Cousin Lou" on 7 July 1863: "We have had the dark hour. The dawn has broken. . . . Bells are ringing wildly all over the city. . . . How I envy the heroes of Meade's Army. It would be worth while to die in order that one's friends might say, 'He died at Gettysburg.' . . . My letter must be short and jubilant. I cannot do anything long today."[1] Lieutenant Lusk's elation spoke for all his comrades in the Army of the Potomac who needed a victory to offset the frustration of repeated defeats by the Army of Northern Virginia during the past year. Almost prophetically Lusk had written his mother on 27 January 1863 that "the Army of the Potomac is splendid in material, and once taught that their best efforts are not to be wasted, they will tell for themselves a splendid story."[2]

Lieutenant Lusk was not marked to fight at Gettysburg, but some 1,300 Connecticut Yankees were, and their casualties were high: 68 men killed or mortally wounded, and 291 wounded, captured, or missing. While Connecticut did not have the largest state contingent there—nor did its men suffer the highest percentage of Union losses—all present were volunteers from a state that had managed without a draft to

[ 1 ]

supply 35,000 men to the Union cause by 1863—more than half of Connecticut's manpower between the ages of 18 and 40.[3] Connecticut's presence, though small, was representative, for, as fate would have it, its five small infantry regiments and one light artillery battery fought in almost every major phase of the battle.

As Connecticut's soldiers joined in the march north toward Pennsylvania in late June 1863, all were aware that somewhere ahead of them were Gen. Robert E. Lee's Army of Northern Virginia. But few could see the larger picture, or guess at Lee's reasons for launching a second invasion of the north. Private Henry F. Prindle of the 5th Connecticut probably mirrored the feelings of his comrades when he wrote his parents on 22 June: "I don't know anything about the rest of the Army outside of this Corps but understand they are around somewhere. There has been no hard fighting yet but expect there will be before long."[4]

Even as Prindle wrote, advanced units of Lee's army had already entered Pennsylvania, and by 28 June some 75,000 Confederates would be scattered from Chambersburg to the west to the Susquehanna River on the east. Meeting little resistance, the Army of Northern Virginia had already succeeded in meeting one of Lee's goals in this invasion—the taking of badly needed supplies. His forces had also marched near Harrisburg, throwing that city into a panic and threatening to destroy the rolling stock and yards of the key east-west railroads that converged there. With his army now strategically placed, Lee felt confident he could force the Army of the Potomac to march north, do battle on his terms, and then suffer a defeat on Northern soil—one that might convince a war-weary Northern public to sue for peace or, at the very least, compel Gen. Ulysses S. Grant to abandon his siege of the Confederate stronghold at Vicksburg, Mississippi, in order to send reinforcements to the Army of the Potomac.[5]

Until the evening of 28 June 1863, Lee had good reason to be pleased with the progress of his army's invasion, though he had been troubled by the lack of any news from his cavalry commander "Jeb" Stuart, who would certainly have warned him if the Union army was turning north in pursuit. That evening, however, a spy employed by Gen. James Longstreet, commander of the First Corps of Lee's army, reported to Longstreet that the Union army had already crossed the Potomac River and that much of its strength was in and near Frederick, Maryland, less than 40 miles from Lee's headquarters at Chambersburg. Moreover, the spy also reported that Gen. Joseph Hooker had been replaced by Gen. George Gordon Meade as commander of the Army of the Potomac.[6]

Though Lee did not know why he had heard nothing from General Stuart, he decided that he could not afford to ignore the news conveyed by Longstreet's spy—no doubt in part because he credited the intelligence that the new commander of the Army of the Potomac was General Meade, an officer for whom he had a great deal more respect than his opponent at Chancellorsville, "Fighting" Joe Hooker. Lee promptly ordered his couriers to carry orders to the scattered units of his army, advising them to concentrate as soon as possible in the area of Cashtown, about 20 miles east of Chambersburg at the foot of South Mountain. Lee knew that time favored the first army that could concentrate and force a battle on favorable terrain. If he consolidated his command before General Meade succeeded in locating his position, he would be able to overwhelm his adversary. For Lee's immediate purpose, then, all roads passed through Gettysburg.

About the time that Lee ordered his army to concentrate near Cashtown, Meade was studying the deployment of the Army of the Potomac. He knew his mission: drive north toward the Susquehanna River and bring Lee to battle. From his headquarters in Frederick, Maryland, one of the best routes to the Susquehanna lay north through Gettysburg, and a network of three roads could be used to push his troops toward that town. During the evening of 29 June, Meade got off a few quick lines to his wife, telling her, "we are marching as fast as we can to relieve Harrisburg. I am going straight at them and will settle this thing one way or another."[7]

Once Meade had learned the disposition of his troops, he quickly realigned them and ordered his seven corps commanders to drive the men more to the north and northeast. By 30 June Meade's orders placed each corps within a day's march of Gettysburg. When he moved his headquarters and that of his Artillery Reserve from Frederick to Taneytown, Maryland, he pushed the other units of his army either across the Pennsylvania line or very close to it. Approaching Gettysburg along the Emmitsburg Road, Maj. Gen. John F. Reynolds's First Corps stopped for the night at Marsh Creek, only five miles to the southwest. Behind Reynolds, and camped near Emmitsburg, were the troops of Gen. Oliver Otis Howard's Eleventh Corps, within 11 miles of Gettysburg. One of the men in Howard's command, Pvt. William H. Warren, captured the urgency of Meade's advance when he wrote in his diary on the evening of 29 June: "Marched all day through the mud & rain—very hard walking, & marched between 21 & 22 miles to Emmitsburg."[8]

Private Warren's regiment was the 17th Connecticut, and when the unit bivouacked near Emmitsburg that evening, it numbered just 17 officers and 369 enlisted men, a far cry from its original strength of nearly 1,000 when it mustered into federal service in Bridgeport less than a year before. Recruited in Fairfield County, the regiment's first commander was Col. William H. Noble of Bridgeport, a friend and business partner of Bridgeport's internationally famous showman, Phineas T. Barnum. Assigned to Howard's Eleventh Corps, the regiment suffered heavy losses at Chancellorsville when Gen. Thomas J. "Stonewall" Jackson overran the Union right flank. Along with the rest of the Eleventh Corps, the regiment retreated in disorder; among its many casualties was Colonel Noble, who was severely wounded, and his second in command, Lt. Col. Charles Walter, also of Bridgeport, who was killed as he and Noble tried to rally the men. As the regiment approached Gettysburg, it was commanded by Lt. Col. Douglas Fowler of Norwalk.[9]

The advance of the five remaining infantry corps of the Army of the Potomac brought more Connecticut regiments closer to Gettysburg. On the evening of 30 June, Maj. Gen. Henry W. Slocum bivouacked his Twelfth Corps near Littlestown, Pennsylvania, 10 miles south of Gettysburg. Brigaded together in the First Division of the Twelfth Corps were the 5th and 20th Connecticut infantry regiments. The veterans of the 5th had been seasoned by several vicious engagements before Chancellorsville, and after that battle carried on its rolls only 221 men of the 1,102 that it had first mustered in Hartford on 23 July 1861. First commanded by Col. Orris S. Ferry, a native of Norwalk and a lawyer-turned-soldier, the regiment drew its strength from every part of the state. When Colonel Ferry gained the rank of brigadier general in March 1862, Col. George G. Chapman of Hartford assumed command. Chapman led the regiment into its bloodiest battle, Cedar Mountain, on 9 August 1862, where he was captured and his successor, Col. Warren W. Packer of Groton, was wounded. Packer convalesced at home and returned to duty in November 1862. By then Colonel Chapman had been exchanged and again commanded the regiment. In late January 1863, Chapman was honorably discharged, and Packer assumed command. Promoted to colonel on 1 March 1863, Packer was captured at Chancellorsville, but he was exchanged in time to lead his regiment at Gettysburg.[10]

When the 20th Connecticut mustered for federal service in New Haven on 8 September 1862, it numbered 981 officers and men. The majority of them came from New Haven, Middlesex, and Hartford counties. Colonel Samuel Ross, a native of Hartford, first commanded the regiment, but prior to Chancellorsville he was placed in command of the Second Brigade of the First Division, Twelfth Corps. Ross was wounded early in the battle and was replaced by Lt. Col. William B. Wooster of Derby, later cited for gallantry in that action. He retained command of the regiment at Gettysburg when the unit numbered just 321 men.[11]

Resting at Uniontown, Maryland, some 22 miles south of Gettysburg, on the evening of 30 June, were two more Connecticut infantry regiments, the 14th and 27th—part of Maj. Gen. Winfield Scott Hancock's Second Corps. Battle scarred at Antietam, Fredericksburg, and Chancellorsville, the 14th Connecticut had been part of the Second Brigade of the Third Division, Second Army Corps since 7 September 1862. Recruited from the state at large, the unit mustered 1,105 men when it entered federal service in Hartford on 23 August 1862. First commanded by Col. Dwight Morris of

Bridgeport, and later by Lt. Col. Sanford H. Perkins of Tor-rington, the 14th then had as its leader Maj. Theodore G. Ellis of Hartford, a civil engineer before the war. When Major Ellis halted his men at Uniontown on the evening of 30 June his ranks numbered just 166 officers and men.[12]

Yet Major Ellis's command more than doubled that of Lt. Col. Henry C. Merwin's 27th Connecticut Infantry. That regiment carried its colors into the Battle of Gettysburg with fewer veterans than any other regiment in Meade's army; only 75 men now marched beneath its banner. When the 27th entered service on 22 October 1862, it numbered 829 men under the command of Col. Richard Bostwick of New Haven. Scheduled for nine months' service, the unit drew most of its recruits from the city of New Haven, with many officers drawn from that city's elite militia unit, the New Haven Grays. Other recruits came from the nearby towns of Branford, Clinton, Guilford, Madison, Milford, Meriden, and Wallingford.[13]

Assigned to the Second Army Corps, the 27th Connecticut came under the leadership of Gen. Winfield Scott Hancock, then commander of the First Division. As part of the Third Brigade and later the Fourth Brigade of that division, the 27th met the Confederates for the first time at Fredericksburg, los-ing in that battle a third of its strength. Later, at Chancellors-ville, most of the regiment found itself surrounded by the Confederates and surrendered. Colonel Bostwick and Lieu-tenant Colonel Merwin were both captured, and as a gesture of defiance towards his captors Merwin ordered his men to burn the fine knapsacks they had been presented by the New Haven Grays before leaving for the front. Because the men of Companies D and F were on detached duty, they es-caped capture at Chancellorsville, and, with another skeleton company formed from men returning from special service or from the hospital, they continued to soldier under the regi-mental colors. Not long after being captured, Colonel Bostwick was paroled, but due to illness he was unable to re-join the regiment. Lieutenant Colonel Merwin received his parole shortly afterward, and he led the unit at Gettysburg.[14]

In addition to the Connecticut infantry regiments approaching Gettysburg, one artillery battery from the Nutmeg State was also in the campaign. On 25 June, the Second Connecticut Light Battery left the defenses of Washington and joined the Artillery Reserve of the Army of the Potomac. Organized in Bridgeport, the battery mustered for service on 10 September 1862. Most of the artillerymen in the unit were drawn from two batteries of the state militia in Bridgeport, and a few more men came from Bridgeport's surrounding towns. Commanded by Capt. John W. Sterling, the battery left Bridgeport with 120 officers and men. When it pulled into the line of march with the Artillery Reserve, 116 men were on the roster. For firepower the battery depended on four James Rifles (firing six-pound projectiles) and two four-pounder howitzers.[15]

The 5th, 14th, 17th, 20th, and 27th infantry regiments and the Second Connecticut Light Artillery thus completed the state's organized contingents in the Gettysburg campaign, and brought a total of 1,285 men to the battle.[16] Some other Connecticut natives were also present in military units from other states or serving in the regiments designated as the "U.S. Regulars," and of the 59 Union generals at Gettysburg, six were either Connecticut-born or had established residence there. First among them ranked Maj. Gen. John Sedgwick, a native of Cornwall, graduate of the United States Military Academy at West Point, and commander of the Sixth Corps, Army of the Potomac. Familiarly known as "Uncle John" to his troops, Sedgwick had faith in Connecticut leadership; two of his generals were also from the Nutmeg State. One was Maj. Gen. Horatio G. Wright, born in Clinton and also a graduate of West Point, where he was later an instructor. He joined Sedgwick's Sixth Corps as commander of the First Division in May 1863 after nearly a year as commander of the Department of the Ohio, headquartered in Cincinnati. The other Connecticut native serving under Sedgwick was Brig. Gen. Alexander Shaler, born in Haddam. Unlike Sedgwick and Wright, Shaler worked his way through the ranks, serving in several New York militia units before the war. Recognized as a good student of military tactics, he was appointed lieutenant colonel of the 65th New York Volunteers in June 1861, and a few months later he became widely known as the author of *Manual of Arms for Light Infantry Using the Rifle Musket.* Promoted to brigadier general on 26 May 1863, Shaler was placed in command of the Third Division of the Sixth Corps.[17]

Serving in the Eleventh Corps under General Howard was Brig. Gen. Adolph von Steinwehr, who was living on a farm near Wallingford, Connecticut, when the war began. Born in Brunswick, Germany, in 1822, he studied at the Brunswick Military Academy and served as an officer in the Prussian Army before coming to the United States during the Mexican War seeking a commission in the U.S. Army. Failing to obtain that, he served with a regiment of Alabama volunteers and then with a group of engineers surveying the new border between the United States and Mexico. He later met and married a woman from Mobile, Alabama, and became an American citizen. At the beginning of the Civil War he was commissioned a colonel in the 29th New York Volunteers and was promoted to brigadier general in October 1861. He led the Second Division of the Eleventh Corps at Gettysburg.[18]

In the Twelfth Corps General Slocum had as a commander of his First Division Brig. Gen. Alpheus S. Williams, born in Saybrook. A Yale graduate (class of 1831), lawyer, judge, and newspaper publisher, Williams served as a lieutenant colonel of the 1st Michigan Volunteers during the Mexican War. Returning to his adopted state of Michigan, Williams was soon promoted to brigadier general of the state militia. In 1859 he achieved the rank of major general and was then commissioned a brigadier general of U.S. Volunteers in May 1861. The sixth Connecticut general present at Gettysburg was Brig. Gen. Robert O. Tyler, commander of the Artillery Reserve. A resident of Hartford, Tyler graduated from West Point in 1853. He spent much of his career as an artillery specialist, and in November 1862 he was raised to the rank of brigadier general.[19]

At about 11 A.M. on 30 June, a Federal cavalry division rode into Gettysburg. Led by the vigorous and aggressive Brig.

Gen. John Buford, the division scouted the area. Buford was convinced that Southern troops were close at hand and that units of Gen. A. P. Hill's Confederate Third Corps were in his vicinity. Couriers brought reports to Meade, who ordered Buford to hold his position near Gettysburg for the night. By the early hours of 1 July 1863, the First, Eleventh, and Twelfth corps were closing in on Gettysburg. General Buford positioned his dismounted cavalry a few miles west of the town to intercept any Confederate attempt to advance along the Chambersburg Pike into Gettysburg. The swords were about to cross, and many a blade would be broken.

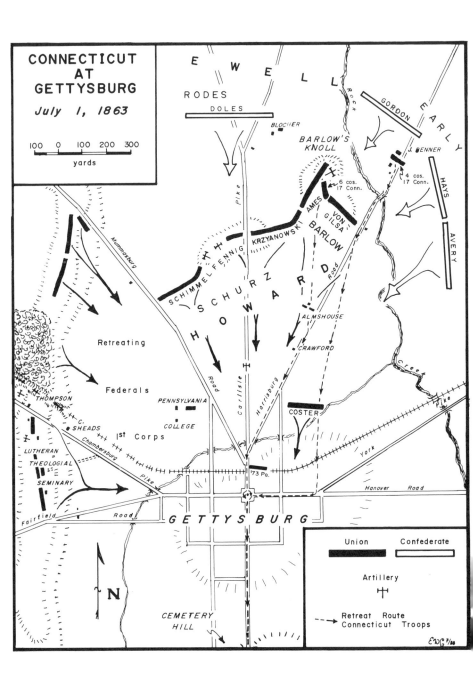

**CONNECTICUT AT GETTYSBURG**

*July 1, 1863*

100  0  100  200  300
yards

E W E L L

RODES

DOLES

BLOCHER

BARLOW'S KNOLL

GORDON

EARLY

J. BENNER

6 cos. 17 Conn.

4 cos. 17 Conn.

HAYS

AVERY

AMES

VON GILSA

BARLOW

SCHIMMELFENNIG

KRZYANOWSKI

SCHURZ

HOWARD

Mummasburg

Road

Pike

Carlisle

Harrisburg

Road

ALMSHOUSE

CRAWFORD

Retreating

Federals

THOMPSON

C. SHEADS

PENNSYLVANIA

COLLEGE

1st Corps

Chambersburg

Pike

COSTER

Creek

Pike

LUTHERAN

THEOLOGIAL

SEMINARY

73 Pa.

York

Hanover  Road

Fairfield

Road

**GETTYSBURG**

N

CEMETERY

HILL

| Union | Confederate |
|:---:|:---:|

Artillery

Retreat Route
Connecticut Troops

EWG 7/88

| "Always | | The 17th |
| Brave and | 2 | Connecticut at |
| Energetic" | | Barlow's Knoll |

And ever the hastening of shifting positions,
Batteries, cavalry, moving hither and thither.
—Walt Whitman, "The Artilleryman's Vision"

ON THE EVENING of 30 June, Southern general Henry Heth's division of Gen. A. P. Hill's Third Corps was positioned at Cashtown. Heth later recalled that when he asked Hill if there was any objection to advancing the division to Gettysburg, Hill replied, "None in the world."[1] What Heth could not know, however, was that his decision would open the first act of one of the greatest dramas of the Civil War. The stage was set by the morning of 1 July, for Northern general John Buford "had gained positive information of the enemy's position and movements, and my [Buford's] arrangements were made for entertaining him until General Reynolds could reach the scene."[2] Buford would indeed keep his antagonist on stage until Maj. Gen. John Fulton Reynolds, in command of the Union left wing, took over the director's role. Reynolds, at Buford's urging, rushed toward the action; both Doubleday's First Corps and Howard's Eleventh Corps marched up Emmitsburg Road not far behind him.

Heth sought to make a "reconnaissance in force" to check on the possibility of Federal cavalry and to secure additional supplies. General Lee wanted no major battle until his army was concentrated, but Heth did not yield center stage. Perhaps vexed by the heavy rifle and carbine fire of Buford's two cavalry brigades, Heth was committed increasingly to using more of his division in what fast became a major battle. When Heth first ordered forward the two brigades under James Archer and Joseph Davis, he moved into battle with about half his men, but Buford's resistance soon proved fierce enough to lead Heth to hesitate and regroup before sending in still more of his 7,500 troops. Buford was then "entertaining" his adversaries with about 2,500 dismounted cavalrymen, each armed with carbines. Buford watched the fight develop from the cupola of the Lutheran Seminary dormitory about a mile west of town along Seminary Ridge. At about 9:00 A.M., General Reynolds reached the seminary, jumped from his horse, and learned from Buford the growing dimensions of the conflict.[3]

Reynolds was a dynamic leader, and his military acumen had previously brought from President Lincoln's office a quiet offer to command the Army of the Potomac, an offer as quietly rejected. A soldier to the core, Reynolds was suspicious of politicians and resented their attempts to control the direction of the army once campaign wheels were in motion. When he took temporary command at Gettysburg, he was subordinate to General Meade, but he was Meade's most respected commander and his friend as well.[4]

Sharp and sure in his decisions, Reynolds dispatched riders to General Doubleday, telling him to take the First Division of his First Army Corps off the Emmitsburg Road and cut northwest across the fields with all possible speed to the Chambersburg Road, coming up behind McPherson's Ridge. A little after 10:00 A.M. Brig. Gen. James S. Wadsworth's two brigades moved into position along that ridge, relieving Buford's tired cavalrymen. Meanwhile, Reynolds got off a quick report to Meade, saying that a strong enemy force was bearing down on Gettysburg from the west and that he would do his best to keep them out of town.[5]

Like Buford, Reynolds recognized the strategic worth of the hill dominating the southern end of town. Known as Cemetery Hill, this eminence was the obvious defensive key to the area if a major battle developed. The army in control of the heights would have a tactical advantage worth any initial casualties, and Reynolds had already determined to hold a defensive position to gain time for the rest of Meade's army to come up. To the west of the immediate action, a picnic area known as Herbst's Woods lay along McPherson's Ridge south of the Chambersburg Pike. As Reynolds helped direct some of Wadsworth's regiments into position near the woods, a Rebel bullet struck him in the head and killed him. He was dead before he slipped out of his saddle.[6] The loss of this gallant leader placed temporary command of all Northern troops then present upon the shoulders of Maj. Gen. Abner Doubleday.

As instructed previously by Reynolds, Doubleday positioned his men across the Chambersburg Pike. When these veteran regiments took position, about 4,000 of the North's best soldiers were ready for the renewed assault. James Archer's Rebel brigade under Heth's command ran up against stubborn resistance from the famous "Iron Brigade" of Wadsworth's First Division, which seized the initiative, charged down the slope of McPherson's Ridge toward Willoughby Run, and captured General Archer and a number of his men. Leading the forward column of the 19th Indiana in that attack was Lt. Col. William W. Dudley, formerly of New Haven. Heth's other Confederate brigade under Joseph Davis soon found itself entangled in a railroad cut just north of the Chambersburg Pike. Though Heth's men suffered heavy casualties as they attacked the Union lines, they dealt out heavy punishment as well. However, Heth was forced to again withdraw and regroup west of McPherson's Ridge. At approximately 11:00 A.M., two more divisions of Doubleday's First Corps reached the field to bolster Wadsworth's ranks. Doubleday quickly fleshed out his defenses along McPherson's Ridge with some of these reinforcements, retaining Brig. Gen. John C. Robinson's Second Division near the seminary grounds as his reserve.[7]

At about noon, the flanking game, a favorite strategem of the Civil War, was played. As if part of a carefully designed plan, Maj. Gen. Robert Rodes's Confederate division began to move around Oak Hill from the north, descending on Gettysburg from the direction of Carlisle. This vanguard of Lt. Gen. Richard Ewell's Second Corps soon moved towards

Doubleday's exposed right flank situated just southwest of Oak Hill. To counter this threat, Doubleday quickly adjusted his own right wing, at the same time looking south toward the Emmitsburg Road for evidence of the approach of Howard's Eleventh Corps. To his relief, they were close at hand, and now his task was to hold his position.

When Meade named John Reynolds commander of the left wing of his army, he placed under his control the First, Third, and Eleventh corps. On the evening of 30 June Reynolds learned from Buford that units of the Confederate army were close to Gettysburg and summoned Gen. Oliver O. Howard to his headquarters along Marsh Creek. Reynolds instructed Howard to move the Eleventh Corps early the next morning from Emmitsburg toward Gettysburg, directly behind the First Corps. These, Reynolds said, were the orders of General Meade, who was still at Taneytown. By 8:00 A.M., 1 July, "the Dutchmen" were on the march. To save time they were to march to Gettysburg by two different routes. Barlow's First Division, including the 17th Connecticut, was to move directly along the Emmitsburg Road; von Steinwehr's Second Division and Schurz's Third Division were to march up the Taneytown Road by way of Horner's Mill. Private Warren of the 17th Connecticut later noted that he "marched 5 or 6 miles without a rest, many of the boys fell out; it was a hard tedious march."[8]

Satisfied that his troops were well on their way, Howard and a few of his staff headed towards Gettysburg, 11 miles distant. By 10:30 A.M. they reached the outskirts of town and could hear the noise of battle to the northwest. There Howard learned from one of Reynolds's staff officers that upon arrival the Eleventh Corps was to stand ready for further orders near what is now called the Peach Orchard, bordering the Emmitsburg Road. Howard then proceeded to Gettysburg to report to Reynolds, scouting the countryside as he rode. He too noticed that Cemetery Hill was "the best defensive position within sight," moved up the hill to confirm his impression, then continued into town. Unable to locate Reynolds, he climbed to the roof of the Fahnestock store on Baltimore Street to scan the countryside. Howard had no knowledge of how the fighting had progressed until an aide, Maj. William Riddle, told him of Reynolds's death, adding that Howard was now "the senior officer on the field."[9] As temporary commander of the left wing of Meade's army, he must fight, whatever the odds, to keep Lee's converging divisions from swarming through Gettysburg and charging up Cemetery Hill.

Howard immediately returned to the top of Cemetery Hill and staked out his headquarters near the entrance to Evergreen Cemetery. Within minutes, Maj. Gen. Carl Schurz rode up the hill ahead of his Third Division. As wing commander, Howard's first order named Schurz temporary commander of the Eleventh Corps, which was to buttress Doubleday's right flank as soon as Schurz could get his troops into position.[10] Schurz sent word out to all Eleventh Corps officers to push their units into Gettysburg "on the double," and he lost no time in sending the advance units of his own Third Division to the northern fringe of the town near Oak Hill. By 12:30 P.M., the Third Division, temporarily commanded by Gen. Alexander Schimmelfennig, stretched a thin defense line across the flat open fields a half mile north of Pennsylvania College. Southern opposition was already strong enough to prevent these regiments from linking up with Doubleday's right flank. General Schurz plugged the gap with two batteries of Eleventh Corps artillery.[11]

After the last regiments of the Third Division had marched through Gettysburg, the men of the 17th Connecticut swung into view, pressing along the Emmitsburg Road with the rest of Brig. Gen. Francis Barlow's First Division. Howard had expected this young firebrand to be first among Eleventh Corps arrivals, but he later noted that "Barlow that day, always vigorous and pushing, owing to the heat of the weather, a road full of ruts and stones, and still obstructed by the supply wagons of the preceding corps, made an average of but two and one-half miles per hour." When Barlow finally got his troops to the edge of town, Howard decided to personally conduct this division to its assigned position—the extreme right of the Federal line. As Howard put it, "I rode with Barlow through the city and out to what is now Barlow Hill." There he left him "to complete his march and deployment near the upper waters of Rock Creek."[12]

At about 2:00 P.M., Brig. Gen. Adolph von Steinwehr made his way to Howard's headquarters for instructions. Howard ordered von Steinwehr to station some of the regiments of his Second Division on the crest of Cemetery Hill where two artillery batteries were already in position. Three more regiments were soon posted along the northern foot of the hill. These troops were to be Howard's reserve, positioned with artillery support to protect that strategic height and to cover the retreat of friendly forces if that became necessary. When Barlow deployed his division on the far right of the Federal line northeast of Gettysburg, he positioned the last of some 9,200 men that Howard had to commit to the first day's fight. On the left side of the defensive arc, Doubleday continued to command what remained of the 8,200 First Corps soldiers. Supporting the flanks of the Northern line were Buford's two cavalry brigades, about 3,000 men at the beginning of the fight early in the day. Altogether, Northern forces committed to the fight on 1 July numbered 20,400 men.[13]

Aware of the growing Confederate strength, Howard repeatedly called for more assistance. Gen. Daniel E. Sickles responded as quickly as he could, but elements of his Third Corps did not reach Gettysburg until 7:00 P.M. General Slocum, on the other hand, refused to move his Twelfth Corps any closer than Two Taverns, an hour's march from Gettysburg. He reasoned that General Meade had warned against bringing on a general engagement, and he was reluctant to commit any of his divisions. Senior to Howard, Slocum would have had to assume command of the entire operation had he moved into the fight. An aide-de-camp to Howard reported that Slocum told him that "he did not wish to come up in person to the front and take the responsibility of that fight."[14] At about 2:00 P.M. Francis Barlow, energetic and eager, pushed his men forward into the line of battle—too far forward, further jeopardizing the already precarious position of Howard's right flank, Barlow's superior officer, Major General Schurz, contended.

Barlow's superiors, Schurz and Howard, considered the options open to them. Standing with Howard atop Cemetery Hill, General Schurz remembered that

> The situation before us was doubtful.... From our point of observation we could perceive but little of the strength of the enemy.... If the enemy before us was only in small force, then we had to push him as far as might seem prudent to General Meade. But if the enemy was bringing on the whole or a large part of his army, ... then we had to look for a strong position in which to establish and maintain ourselves until reinforced or ordered back.[15]

Surge forward or stand on the defensive. The decision was Howard's. He chose to go on the offensive, to play his card in the flanking game. If he could get around Dole's Confederate brigade now forcing its way south from the Oak Hill area, he could relieve the increasing pressure on Doubleday's First Corps line. Howard recalled: "I ordered the 1st and 3rd Divisions to seize and hold a prominent height on the right of the Cashtown Road and on the prolongation of Seminary Ridge, each division to have a battery of artillery ... "[16] The prominent height was Oak Hill, and to get Barlow's First Division into a position to help seize that hill, Howard acted as personal escort. Barlow then occupied the knoll, which now bears his name, under Howard's personal direction.

General Schurz indicated otherwise. He wanted Barlow to anchor his right flank at the old Alms House on the Harrisburg Road, a stronger defensive position in his view. But contrary to those orders, Barlow advanced to the knoll, compounding Schurz's defensive problems. As Schurz put it, "I now noticed that Barlow, be it that he had misunderstood my order, or that he was carried away by the ardor of the conflict, had advanced his whole line and lost connection with my Third Division on his left, and in addition to this, he had instead of refusing, pushed forward his right brigade, so that it formed a projecting angle with the rest of the line."[17]

The day was hot and sultry as the 17th Connecticut marched into Gettysburg. While passing through the lower end of town, Private Warren noted that "the citizens stood in their doors handing us water and victuals." The unit then headed north, halting briefly "in a meadow by the road [Harrisburg Road] close column in mass for a rest."[18] Brig. Gen. Adelbert Ames commanded the Second Brigade of Barlow's division. When he learned from Barlow the general area to be occupied by the Second Brigade, Ames immediately sent one of his aides, Lt. Charles E. Doty of Norwalk, formerly of Company F, 17th Connecticut, to request that a detachment of the 17th proceed as rapidly as possible along the Harrisburg Road to secure a small wooden bridge spanning Rock Creek. Then, as skirmishers, they were to press across the bridge in order to take and hold "a brick house to the left and beyond the bridge." Lieutenant Colonel Fowler called for volunteers, and Maj. Allen G. Brady, second in command of the regiment, offered to lead them. In the words of Lieutenant Doty: "Captain Henry Allen, then in command of Company F, at once stepped forward, and saluting, said: 'Colonel Fowler, Company F is ready.' " Other volunteers quickly stepped forward, and as Major Brady set out on his mission he had with him Companies A, B, F, and K commanded, respectively, by Captains John McQuade of Norwalk, Charles A. Hobbie of Darien, Henry Allen of Norwalk, and John J. McCarty of Fairfield.[19] These Connecticut infantry, once across the bridge, were at the extreme right of the entire Federal line. They were the only organized units during the first day's fight to engage the Confederates on the far side of Rock Creek.

The rest of Barlow's division followed along the Harrisburg Road toward Rock Creek to the Alms House. Here Schurz expected Barlow to ground his right flank behind the protective brick walls of the buildings on the grounds. But it was not long before Lt. Bayard Wilkeson, commanding Battery G, 4th United States Artillery, wheeled four of his Napoleon cannons to the only elevation near the Alms House, the hillock about 500 yards northeast bordering on Rock Creek. It was the best site in the area for artillery, and Barlow thought that

Wilkeson would also need infantry support to maintain his position. Furthermore, he was in the mood to take his turn in the flanking game. These were his orders as viewed by General Howard, and by swinging his 3,200 men up the gentle slope of the knoll and then into battle line, he could send them down the opposite side in a northwesterly direction and slam into the left flank of Dole's Georgia brigade. At the same time he could give Wilkeson's guns the infantry support they needed. As Barlow's men moved up the knoll, Confederate skirmishers in the area were speedily swept aside. A little before 3:00 P.M. Barlow had his two brigades on top of and along the eastern and northern slopes of the knoll. Already Wilkeson had zeroed in on two Southern batteries located on the eastern edge of Oak Hill.[20]

On the first day at Gettysburg, Col. Leopold von Gilsa, Barlow's First Brigade commander, had only three regiments available for fighting. Another, the 41st New York, was still at Emmitsburg on detached duty. As the tempo of the artillery fire increased, von Gilsa placed his regiments along the bank of Rock Creek footing the knoll. The 54th New York held down the right of von Gilsa's line near the bridge, and on the left of the 54th were the 68th New York and 153d Pennsylvania in that order.[21] Where the hillock rounded toward the north and northwest, General Ames, commanding the Second Brigade, butted his regiments against von Gilsa's. First in line were the troops of the 25th Ohio. On the left of that regiment Lieutenant Colonel Fowler readied the six remaining companies of the 17th Connecticut. His line was extended to the left by first the 75th and then the 107th Ohio regiments. Nestled among these units at the highest point of the knoll, Lieutenant Wilkeson's guns fired at the enemy as rapidly as his sweating gunners could load them. The heavy Confederate return fire made some of the Nutmeggers uneasy, prompting Lieutenant Colonel Fowler to jokingly cry out: "Dodge the big ones, boys!"[22]

Barlow was ready to make his move. Colonel von Gilsa already had skirmishers moving north along the creek side to feel out the Confederate left flank. Dole was pushing his Georgians slowly toward Gettysburg just to the left of

Barlow's battle line. So intent was Barlow upon attacking Dole that he did not heed the military lightning flashing on his own right, directly across the creek.

On the opposite side of Rock Creek the four Connecticut companies were getting more than their share of Confederate attention as they approached the two-story brick home of Josiah Benner. Their leader, Maj. Allen G. Brady of Torrington, pugnacious and controversial, had twice been passed over for a regimental command. He had first entered service on 7 May 1861 as lieutenant colonel of the 3d Connecticut Volunteers, a 90-day regiment. The regiment soon moved to Washington with Brady as its executive officer. There, his regimental commander, Col. John Arnold, "not having proved very efficient," resigned and returned to Connecticut. Brady expected promotion to command, but Connecticut governor William Buckingham gave the post to Lt. Col. John L. Chatfield, transferring him from the 1st Connecticut Volunteer Regiment. An incensed Brady "refused to recognize Colonel Chatfield as his superior," and for his insubordination he was "deprived of his sword." This polite phrasing covers the fact that Brady "was placed under arrest for mutiny, and so held without trial, until the final muster out."[23] Since the 3d Connecticut Regiment was committed to but three months' service, Brady was released on 12 August 1861.

But soldiering was in Brady's blood. Accepted for duty with the 17th Connecticut, he reentered service on 18 July 1862 as captain of Company B, and on 29 August of that year was promoted to major. At Chancellorsville Confederate fire severely wounded the commander, Col. William H. Noble, and killed Lt. Col. Charles Walter, second in command. Once again, Major Brady, in line for regimental command, was passed over; Capt. Douglas Fowler of Company A was promoted to lieutenant colonel and moved in to lead the regiment. This time Brady accepted his fate with more grace and remained with his regiment as its executive officer.

As Brady's Nutmeggers approached the Benner Farm, "two companies were thrown out, and deployed as skirmishers as rapidly as possible to the right of the bridge, along the creek. The other two, held as reserve, were advanced in line, loading

Fig. 1. Maj. Gen. John Sedgwick. Photograph reprinted from *Dedication of the Equestrian Statue of Major-General John Sedgwick* (1913).

Fig. 2. Maj. Allen G. Brady, 17th Connecticut. Courtesy Bridgeport
Public Library, Bridgeport, Conn.

Fig. 3. Lt. Col. Douglas Fowler, 17th Connecticut. Courtesy
Bridgeport Public Library.

Fig. 4. Gen. Adolph von Steinwehr. Courtesy *MOLLUS*.

Fig. 5. Gen. Robert O. Tyler. Courtesy *MOLLUS*.

Fig. 6. Gen. Alpheus Williams. Courtesy *MOLLUS*.

Fig. 7. Josiah Benner farmhouse (ca. 1870). Courtesy W. E. Jordan.

Fig. 8. Josiah Benner barn and outbuildings (ca. 1870).
Courtesy W. E. Jordan.

and firing as rapidly as possible, making at the same time a left wheel, so as to swing our right around the house, the reserve keeping near and conforming to the movements of the skirmishers." Here they drew fire from the Confederate artillery and Southern skirmishers. Brady tells of the enemy pouring in "shot, shell, grape, and canister." The concentration of fire was effective enough to slow down the advance toward the buildings, so much so that "Major Brady, dismounted, went in front of the line of skirmishers, and led them on until quite near the house."[24] Aware of Brady's desire to use the buildings for protection, the Confederates trained their guns on the farmhouse, and soon portions of it caught fire. But, said Brady, "We held our ground, and held the enemy's skirmishers in check." He added in his battle report that most of his men were excellent marksmen and had volunteered for this mission. Brisk fighting continued until General Ames ordered Brady to "draw in his skirmishers and return to town as rapidly as possible."[25]

Ames had good reason to recall Brady's men. Barlow, poised on his knoll and ready to cut into Dole's left flank, was about to drive his regiments forward. Doubleday, whose First Corps was then very much in need of Barlow's assistance, said,

Barlow had advanced with Von Gilsa's brigade, had driven back Ewell's skirmish line, and with the aid of Wilkeson's battery was preparing to hold the Carlisle Road. He was not aware that Early was approaching, and saw Dole's advance with pleasure, for he felt confident he could swing around his right and envelop Dole's left; a manoeuvre which could hardly fail to be successful.

But General Howard stopped him. As he phrased it, "Barlow against a shower of bullets made a strong effort to advance his lines, but as soon as I heard of the approach of Ewell and saw that nothing could prevent the turning of my right flank if Barlow advanced, the order was countermanded, except to press out a skirmish line."[26]

Barlow seems not to have sensed the danger. Intent on pressing his attack on Dole, he and his two brigades suddenly heard the thunder of Gen. Jubal A. Early's division artillery. Less than a half-mile further north on the Harrisburg Road, cannoneers of Lt. Col. H. P. Jones's battalion quickly found the range and fired upon Barlow's exposed right flank. Bombarded from two directions, from Oak Hill and the Harrisburg Road, Lieutenant Wilkeson's four Napoleons on the knoll now returned fire both ways. The concentration of Southern fire on the knoll soon succeeded in knocking this gallant young artilleryman from his horse. As Wilkeson lay mortally wounded, Lt. Eugene A. Bancroft took command of the battery.[27] And while the Southern cannons were weakening the defenses surrounding Barlow's Knoll, Early's entire division moved forward. At about 3:30 P.M. Early had deployed three of his brigades into battle line on the opposite side of Rock Creek, and 6,300 Rebels stood ready to wade across the stream and roll up General Howard's right flank. Theirs was to be the closing trick of the first day's flanking game.

Leading Early's right brigade was Brig. Gen. John B. Gordon. One of the South's most colorful leaders, Gordon was keen of mind and bold in strategy and was the epitome of the Southern gentleman. His immediate chore was to close ranks with his fellow Georgians in Dole's brigade off to his right near the Carlisle Road and force Barlow off the knoll, a dramatic entry into action.

The Union forces . . . were again advancing and pressing back Lee's left and threatening to envelop it. The Confederates were stubbornly contesting every foot of ground, but the Southern left was slowly yielding. A few moments more and that day's battle might have been ended by the complete turning of Lee's flank. I was ordered to move at once to the aid of the heavily pressed Confederates. With a ringing yell my command rushed upon the line posted to protect the Union right.[28]

Caught in the confusion of changing fronts to meet this new threat were the six companies of the 17th Connecticut.

When General Gordon turned his Georgians loose, a full brigade of Rebels came out of the wheat fields, crossed the creek, and broke into the open area at the foot of the knoll. Within minutes the charging Confederates had flushed out and sent over the hillock the remnants of von Gilsa's three regiments, previously positioned along the creek. Thrown first into disarray and then into panic, these same unlucky "Dutchmen" were the first troops to "run for it" at Gettysburg, as they were at Chancellorsville. As Gordon chased von Gilsa's men to the rear, he ran into real resistance as his Georgians approached the top of the knoll. Changing front as best it could, Barlow's Second Brigade, under General Ames, made a stubborn fight of it. They were further handicapped, Ames reported, by "the men of the First Brigade of this division running through the lines of the regiments of my Brigade and thereby creating considerable confusion." Private Warren also noted in his diary that "the dutchmans run right through our regt. and broke us up."[29]

Barlow, now with but four fighting regiments, fought to hold his ground against increasing odds. Close by, Lt. Col. Douglas Fowler moved his Connecticut companies toward the on-rushing Confederates. A native of Norwalk, Fowler had been in and out of the army three times since the beginning of the war. Among the first of Connecticut's volunteers, he served first as captain of Company G, 3d Connecticut, until that unit's three months of service expired. In September 1861 he was back in the service with the 8th Connecticut as captain of Company H, which he had raised in and about Norwalk. Fowler resigned his commission in January 1862 and reenlisted as captain of Company A, 17th Connecticut, in July 1862. At Chancellorsville, he left his sickbed to lead his company; he fought tenaciously and was among the last to retreat. Skillful as a tactician, Fowler brought to Gettysburg a regiment of Nutmeggers confident in his ability and ready to follow wherever he led.[30]

From his position on the right of the Union line at the top of the knoll, Fowler prepared for action. In the words of Lieutenant Doty, "Colonel Fowler at once rode to the front and gave the command to deploy columns, and swinging his sword, said: 'Now Seventeenth, do your duty! Forward, double quick! Charge bayonets!' And with a yell, which our boys knew how to give, they charged." When his soldiers approached the top of the rise, a hand-to-hand struggle followed, with the "colors on the two lines being part of the time only fifty paces apart." Mounted conspicuously on a white horse, Fowler was an easy target, and as Private Warren noted in gruesome detail, "Lieut. Colonel Fowler was killed, his head shot off and his brains flew on the Adjutent [H. Whitney Chatfield]." Along with Fowler, "Captain [James E.] Moore was killed about this time, and Captain [Wilson] French and Lieutenant [Henry] Quien were wounded, and many of the men were killed, wounded, and taken prisoners."[31] Barlow's position grew desperate, for in addition to Gordon's Georgians two additional Confederate brigades were beginning to curl in upon the Union flank. With 4,500 Confederates closing in, Barlow had to withdraw or face entrapment. Still unwilling to yield his position, he tried to rally his regiments as they began to move back from the knoll, but at this point he was severely wounded and General Ames assumed command. General Gordon described it this way:

> That protecting Union line once broken left my command not only on the right flank, but obliquely in rear of it. Any troops that were ever marshalled would, under like conditions, have been as surely and swiftly, shattered. There was no alternative for Howard's men except to break and fly, or to throw down their arms and surrender. Under the concentrated fire from front and flank, the marvel is that any escaped.[32]

Some Northern units did "break and fly" from Barlow's Knoll, but it is also true that Ames's Second Brigade and Lieutenant Bancroft's Battery G, 4th U.S. Artillery left the hillock in reasonably good order. Under the command of General Ames, "the division retreated to a second position near the Almshouse, where it formed again." One of those caught up in the retreat was Sgt. Maj. C. Frederick Betts of Norwalk, who first tried to lift the body of Lieutenant Colonel Fowler onto Adjutant Chatfield's horse. In spite of assistance from another soldier, however, "found it impossible to do so, as his weight was beyond our strength, and after several attempts we reluctantly left him." With the enemy closing in, and making requests to surrender "more vigorous than polite," Betts made good his escape by "scaling a fence in front of us [and tearing] across the next field towards the stone wall of the poorhouse."[33] Another soldier who ran for the Almshouse, Private Warren, described in vivid detail those moments in his diary:

> I partly loaded with my back to the enemy, then they commenced to run again so I run—a little ways fother & Rufus Warren fell, he was about a rod ahead of me, he fell the opposite way he was running then throwed up his hands and hollowed *O Dear, Help me, Help me*, it was not time for me to stop so I kept on before I had hard gone a rod fother a bullet cut a hole out of my pants . . . but did not touch me . . . bullets were comeing in a shower I thought I was spoke for, still kept moveing on and shortly I expect it was a piece of spent shell struck my right shoulder blade and almost knocked me over . . . I ran across the field and everything before me looked as white as a sheet . . . [34]

Once at the Almshouse, General Ames ordered Major Brady to "return to town as rapidly as possible, and take command" of the isolated 17th Connecticut still skirmishing near the Benner house. Brady then drew in his skirmishers and pulled back across Rock Creek. Under fire all the way, Brady reported, "we fell back in good order, skirmishing with the enemy, who advanced as we retreated, and tried to cut us off and capture us before we got to the town."[35]

Moving across the creek and toward the town in pursuit of the Connecticut companies, Confederate general Harry T. Hays spurred on his brigade of 1,500 Louisiana Tigers. Hays reported that when General Gordon "encountered the enemy in force, I received an order to advance in support. Pressing steadily on, I met with no other opposition than that presented by the enemy's skirmishers and the firing of artillery." Hays thus agreed with Brady that his advance, ordered to support Gordon's left flank, met no infantry opposition other than Brady's four companies of Connecticut skirmishers. When his advance approached the Almshouse, Hays "found the enemy in considerable strength." There he met the line of resistance hastily prepared by Ames with his Second Brigade remnants. Ames could not withstand for long the overwhelming pressure of the Louisiana Tigers cutting into his flank as Gordon continued to pound him from the front. After crashing into this last organized but feeble Northern defense, General Hays said he continued to move on, "driving before me all the force opposed until I arrived at the railroad . . . just striking the edge of the city of Gettysburg." But Major Brady, a wily, resourceful Yankee, somehow got his four Connecticut companies beyond the embrace of the Confederate encircling arm. "We foiled them . . . by making a circuit and entering the town near the upper end, and soon joined the remainder of the regiment, which we found near the lower end of town."[36]

About the time that General Gordon sent his Georgians splashing across Rock Creek, General Lee caught his first sight of the battlefield. Until that moment he had been anxious about the increasing fury of the fighting ahead of him. He knew long before he came upon the scene that more than a reconnaissance in force had developed. Against his wishes, a full-scale battle was underway. In spite of the haphazard nature of the developing conflict, Lee saw that his army was in an excellent position to win a substantial victory. Directly opposite Lee's position, Early's division was pushing toward Gettysburg from the east, driving Ames's troops before him. From the north, Rodes's division pushed relentlessly south toward town. All Lee had to do was unleash the full strength of William Dorsey Pender's fresh division of the Third Corps to aid Heth's brigades in breaking Doubleday's left flank west of Gettysburg. Lee did not hesitate. He ordered Heth and Pender to hit Doubleday's First Corps with all the strength at hand.

Punished severely all day, Doubleday's troops could not withstand the pounding of this latest stroke and began to pull back toward Seminary Ridge.[37]

As the Southern divisions tightened the vise, the outnumbered Union troops were steadily compressed toward the center of Gettysburg. Howard's right flank collapsed first, leaving Doubleday's rear unprotected. Under intense pressure from Heth and Pender, the First Corps followed the retreat of the Eleventh Corps through the town, jamming its streets and alleys in an effort to move south to Cemetery Hill. Many of these men lost their will to fight and much of their cohesion as the Rebels closed in. Yet there was some resistance as a few Northern units tried momentarily to make a stand. Somehow Major Brady got his Connecticut Yankees to attempt to slow the Southern pursuit. As he rallied his tired men, his efforts caught the eye of a Union soldier retreating through town with the 88th Pennsylvania Regiment:

> Any attempt to make a stand in this bewildered and frantic mob was attended with the greatest difficulty and peril, yet many fragments of both Corps did their level best to breast the storm and repulse the greybacks. Amidst all the excitement, the 17th Connecticut deployed in the streets, firing several rounds before it was compelled to fall back . . . the crowd was frightful and the men almost prostrated with over-exertion and the great heat, while the Confederate sharpshooters occupied the streets . . . their line of battle almost encircling the city.[38]

This account gives credence to Major Brady's report about his efforts to stall the Confederate advance through town. Having located the rest of the regiment in Gettysburg, Brady first reported to General Ames for instructions.

> The enemy were at this time advancing rapidly through the town. The regiment was immediately deployed through the streets, and fired several volleys into the

ranks of the enemy, which thinned their ranks and retarded their advance. We kept the enemy from advancing through the town until ordered to clear the street of our men for the purpose of planting a battery. The battery not being placed in position as intended, and the regiment being in line on the sidewalk, the enemy took advantage of this, and with a superior force rushed through the main street, which compelled us to fall back, which we did reluctantly, but not without contesting the ground inch by inch.[39]

All afternoon General Howard had hesitated to send any reserves from the top of Cemetery Hill to aid the withdrawal of the Northern forces. Almost too late, he allowed General von Steinwehr to send Col. Charles R. Coster's brigade and one artillery battery to the northeastern rim of town to ward off the fast approach of the Confederate brigades led by General Hays and Colonel Avery. Since overrunning the Northern defense line near the Almshouse, Hays had moved ahead unmolested, and Avery's brigade to his left also moved quickly to flank the Eleventh Corps. Luckily, Colonel Coster got his brigade into position beyond the railroad station in town just before the Southerners closed in. Coster's brigade fought stubbornly and long enough to allow many Union soldiers to get through the town to Cemetery Hill. Protected by this temporary screen, General Ames's First Division was able to withdraw.[40]

Close behind Ames's First Division, the shattered ranks of General Schimmelfennig's Third Division of the Eleventh Corps intermingled with Doubleday's First Corps troops now streaming through town. As these Union soldiers scrambled toward Cemetery Hill, the Rebels jammed into town from the east, the north, and the west. Every street echoed rifle fire and the boisterous Rebel yells of Lee's victorious men. Casualties were high among the Union soldiers, and thousands of Federal infantrymen were taken prisoner as their lanes of escape collapsed. The melee in and about town was so confused, though, that the Confederate surge lost its momentum. When General Ewell reached the center of Gettysburg, he observed a state of jubilation and disorder among his own troops so great that any organized pursuit of the fleeing Yankees was at that moment impossible. Precious moments were lost as Ewell reorganized his men for an assault on Cemetery Hill. A discretionary order from Lee suggested a prompt move against the hills to the south of Gettysburg, but Ewell chose not to move. His work for the day was done. His hesitation gave Howard's men precious minutes to regroup for the defense of their hilltop.[41]

As some of Brady's veterans climbed to the top of Cemetery Hill, General Howard, unaware that they were Connecticut men, approached the men, taking them for one of his German regiments. Howard remembered

Seeing the color sergeant and guard as they came between me and the stone wall, near the edge of the city, I called out: "Sergeant, plant your flag down there in that stone wall!" Not recognizing me the sergeant said impulsively: "All right, if you will go with me, I will!" Whereupon I took the flag and accompanied by Rogers Howard's aide the sergeant and his men, set it above the wall. That flag served to rally the regiment, always brave and energetic, and other troops.

Major Brady's official report of the same incident, written on 4 July 1863, said:

About this time Major General Howard, who was in the thickest of the battle, regardless of danger, asked if he had troops brave enough to advance to a stone wall across a lot toward the town, and said he would lead them. We replied "Yes, the Seventeenth Connecticut will," and advanced at once to the place indicated, remained a few moments, and again advanced across another lot still nearer the town and behind a rail-fence at the upper end of the town, which position we held until late in the evening, exposed to a galling fire from the enemy's sharpshooters.[42]

While the 17th Connecticut and a few other Union regiments protected the escape route to Cemetery Hill, Northern soldiers able to break free from the havoc in town struggled up the slope toward Howard's headquarters. On the crest, Howard and his aides continued efforts to reorganize the new arrivals and post them in positions to ward off any sudden Confederate attack. At 4:30 P.M. Second Corps commander Maj. Gen. Winfield Scott Hancock and his staff arrived, sent ahead by General Meade to take temporary command at Gettysburg. Because Howard was senior to Hancock in rank, Hancock's assumption of command initially caused friction between the generals, but the shared chores of setting up the defenses of Cemetery Hill helped ease the tension.[43]

Once Hancock was on the scene, he lifted the spirits of all around him; he was a commander whose presence and ability called forth immediate respect and trust. Within minutes of his arrival, his direction brought gradual order out of what had been milling confusion. Soon the Federals on Cemetery Hill, and further to the east on Culp's Hill, were fortifying already strong defensive positions. When Hancock was satisfied that the Confederates would not attack that evening, he sent word to Meade that Gettysburg was the place to fight Lee. When Meade arrived early the next morning to take command, he informed the tired defenders of the hill that his entire army would be at Gettysburg before the end of the following day.[44]

The first day at Gettysburg had been costly for the more than 20,000 Union soldiers who reached the field; 9,100 were casualties before evening. But their sacrifice had interrupted Lee's original plans, exacted thousands of Confederate casualties, and given Meade the advantage of defending the strategic heights south of town on the following day. Were it not for the stubborn resistance of the left wing of the Army of the Potomac that day, General Lee might well have turned Gettysburg into another Chancellorsville—but with far more serious consequences.

When Major Brady mustered the 17th Connecticut on the morning of 2 July, only 241 men answered roll call. The regiment had lost 145 of its 386 men: 17 killed, 73 wounded, and

55 missing or captured. Nine of these casualties were among the four companies—A, B, F, and K—detached from the regiment as skirmishers at the Benner Farm, where three men were killed, two wounded, and four captured.[45] The regiment suffered another 136 casualties during the fight at Barlow's Knoll, the short encounter at the Almshouse, and the final retreat through town. One of those casualties, Private Justus Silliman of New Canaan, a member of Company H, described to his mother the circumstances that led to his wounding and capture at Barlow's Knoll:

> My gun would not work so I dropped it and picked up another. This also missed fire (it had rained in the morning). Just then a man near me was shot. I seized his gun and had just fired at some rebs advancing on our left when I experienced a curious sensation in the head. On opening my eyes I found myself in a horizontal position and surrounded by Greybacks, our men having been forced back a short distance. I placed my cartridge box in front of my bruised noodle and lay a short time. Was then sent to a rebel hospital about three miles to the rear.[46]

Though the regiment lost 38 percent of its strength on the first day of the battle, the 17th Connecticut continued the fight on the following evening. By chance, they faced Hay's Louisiana Tigers once more. These were the same soldiers that had sent the Nutmeggers scurrying on 1 July, but toward dusk on 2 July quite a different story unfolded.

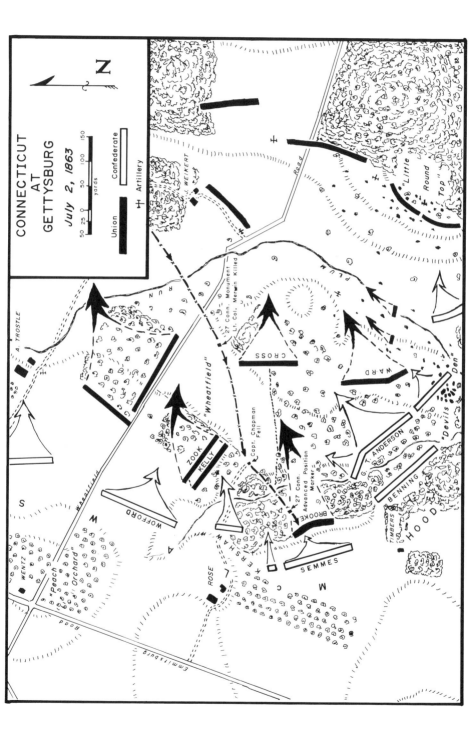

CONNECTICUT
AT
GETTYSBURG

*July 2, 1863*

yards

50  25  0      50      100     150

Union

Confederate

Artillery

N

# "My Poor Regiment"

# 3

# The 27th Connecticut & the Wheat Field Fight

There is a peach orchard there, a field of ripe wheat and other peaceable things soon not to be peaceable.
—Stephen Vincent Benét, *John Brown's Body*

IN THE LATE AFTERNOON of 2 July, Lt. Frank Haskell, aide to Brig. Gen. John Gibbon, stared toward the southwest from his Union position on the crest of Cemetery Hill. Fascinated by the sights and sounds below, Haskell captured the fury of the fight when he wrote: "O the din and the roar, and these thirty thousand Rebel wolf cries! What a hell is there down that valley!" Caught in that hell were the men of the 27th Connecticut. These Yankees wrote their names indelibly on that part of the battleground known as the Wheat Field. Along with thousands of other Federal troops, they fought there because Maj. Gen. Daniel E. Sickles chose to advance his Third Corps line along the Emmitsburg Road without the consent of General Meade.[1] How they got there is the story that follows.

Early on 1 July, after the Second Corps had bivouacked near Unionville, General Hancock moved troops along the road north toward Taneytown. The corps arrived at about 11:00 A.M., and Hancock halted, awaiting further orders. Resting with the corps were two Connecticut regiments—the 14th, assigned to Brigadier General Hays's Third Division, and the 27th, a part of Brigadier General Caldwell's First Division.

Around noon on 1 July, Meade learned from a courier that General Reynolds had been killed. Stunned by the loss,

Meade ordered General Hancock to rush forward and take command at Gettysburg. Brig. Gen. John Gibbon then assumed temporary command of the Second Corps, and by 2:00 P.M. he had the three infantry divisions of the corps trudging north toward Gettysburg. All of Meade's army were homing in on Gettysburg, if not already there. The First and Eleventh corps were heavily engaged, and the Twelfth was just four miles away at Two Taverns. The Third Corps was marching up the Emmitsburg Road from the southwest, and the Fifth and Sixth corps were fast approaching from the southeast. Sure of the hunting grounds of his Confederate quarry, General Meade lost no time in forcing General Lee to stand at bay.[2]

When the leading division of the Second Corps reached the outskirts of Gettysburg, dusk mantled the nearby fields and hills and the noise of the first day's battle had subsided. The Second Division, leading the column, drew off to the left of the Taneytown Road as it neared Big Round Top, a high hill some three miles south of town. The other two divisions were close behind and took positions nearby. The men settled in for the night; they entrenched their positions, ate sparse rations, and stretched out under the stars or under makeshift shelters. These were veteran troops, and they knew what tomorrow might bring. But some could not seek the luxury of a few hours sleep, and among those were the men of the 14th Connecticut, who were marched out at 10:00 P.M. to do picket duty along the Baltimore Pike. There they remained until the next morning at daybreak, when they were ordered to rejoin their brigade.[3] Their companions in the 27th Connecticut were a little more fortunate and managed to get some rest before the corps moved forward shortly after 3:00 A.M. to its designated area in the Union line along the crest of Cemetery Ridge.

For the first time in many encounters with the Army of Northern Virginia, the Army of the Potomac now held ground advantageous for defense, for the valiant efforts of the First and Eleventh corps made it possible for Meade to concentrate his army on the heights south of Gettysburg. When Meade arrived early on the morning of 2 July, he surveyed the terrain, liking what he saw and agreeing with Hancock and Howard that these were the hills to fortify. About a half-mile to the southeast of Cemetery Hill, was Culp's Hill, and Hancock and Howard agreed that Culp's Hill, footed by Rock Creek along its eastern base, was a natural anchor for that extension of the Union line. In fact, the hill and swale separating it from Cemetery Hill was already occupied by General Slocum's Twelfth Corps and some of the remnants of General Doubleday's First Corps, now commanded by Gen. John Newton. Since retreating to Cemetery Hill, Howard's Eleventh Corps occupied the eastern and northern faces of that height.[4] To the west and south of Cemetery Hill's gently sloping ridge were two more hills—Little Round Top was the nearer, ledged and craggy, and a half-mile beyond was Big Round Top. These were two natural bastions to protect the left flank of a defensive line stretching along Cemetery Ridge. Hancock had already occupied Little Round Top, securing it with detachments from General Slocum's Twelfth Corps. Now Meade had only to get into line along Cemetery Ridge enough infantry and artillery to withstand whatever Confederate assault Lee planned for the following day. Fortunately, he had the troops at hand to maintain that line.

Confident that his army possessed a strong defensive position, Meade established his headquarters at the home of the widow Lydia Leister, whose small frame farmhouse stood halfway down the slope of Cemetery Ridge on the Taneytown Road. Quickly and decisively, Meade sent orders out to all corps commanders. At dawn Hancock's Second Corps, now led by General Gibbon, moved from its bivouac near Big Round Top and up the slope of Cemetery Hill by way of the Taneytown Road. When its leading division reached the area defended by Lt. George A. Woodruff's battery on the northwest shoulder of the hill, all three divisions of the corps turned left from the road and assumed positions along Cemetery Ridge facing west.

Sgt. Maj. William B. Hincks of Bridgeport, a member of Company A, 14th Connecticut remembered that on the early morning of 2 July

The mist hung thick and heavy over the ground. We were recalled from the picket line soon after dawn and followed a narrow and rugged road which gradually ascended toward the front. After we had marched perhaps a couple of miles . . . we turned off from the road to the left, and after going up a little ascent, the brigade was halted in column by regiments on a grassy field or plateau of considerable size.[5]

Sergeant Hincks also noted that Woodruff's regular battery of brass pieces was located "a little in advance of us and to our left, in a grove of trees." Directly behind the Third Division, which included the 14th, marched the Second Division of the Second Corps, and finally the 27th Connecticut turned into the field to the left of the Taneytown Road with other units of the First Division commanded by Gen. John Caldwell. Consequently, when Caldwell's men moved into line along Cemetery Ridge, their position was on the extreme left of the Second Corps.

Lieutenant Haskell was meticulous in describing the posting of the Second Corps divisions, for in his words "they were works that I assisted to perform." He noted that when General Hays's Third Division moved into line at the left of the Eleventh Corps, and faced west, the remaining elements of the Second Corps extended the line about a half mile "due south towards Round Top." He was specific in detailing the formations along the front. "The line of the Corps, exclusive of its reserves, was the length of six regiments deployed, . . . and consisted of four common deployed lines, each of two ranks of men, and a little more than one-third over in reserve . . . one hundred and fifty paces in the rear of the line of their respective divisions." Thus, when Caldwell's First Division formed on the left flank of the Second Corps, his troops were deployed in "columns of regiments by brigades." Caldwell's right brigade, as the division pulled into line, was commanded by Col. John R. Brooke. This was the Fourth Brigade and included the 27th Connecticut, 2d Delaware, 64th New York, 53d Pennsylvania, and 145th Pennsylvania.[6]

Once on line the soldiers of the Second Corps took advantage of whatever protection the terrain afforded. A few stone walls provided some shelter, and here and there a fence offered the beginnings of a breastwork. Lieutenant Haskell caught the mood of the Second Corps veterans as he described their settling in along Cemetery Ridge.

The men stacked their arms—in long bristling rows that stood along the crests—and were at ease. Some men pulled down the rail fences near them and piled them up for breast-works in their front. Some loitered, some went to sleep upon the ground, some, a single man carrying twenty canteens slung over his shoulder, went for water. Some made them a fire and boiled a dipper of coffee. Some with knees cocked up, enjoyed the soldier's peculiar solace, a pipe of tobacco. Some were mirthful and chatty, and some were serious and silent.[7]

When General Sickles's Third Corps moved from its evening bivouac to Cemetery Ridge, it positioned itself on the left of General Caldwell's First Division of the Second Corps. The Union defensive positions reached down Cemetery Ridge to the base of Little Round Top. While Sickles positioned his troops on the ridge, General Sykes brought the leading elements of his Fifth Corps on the scene by way of the Baltimore Pike. Meade decided that Sykes's men would serve as a ready reserve and ordered that it be massed along the Baltimore Pike.[8] From that position, supporting units of the corps could move quickly to any part of the Union line if the Confederates forced the fighting to a point requiring additional Federal strength. This precautionary move later, as the battle progressed, paid Meade high dividends.

Meanwhile, the Artillery Reserve rumbled into the area. Commanded by Brig. Gen. Robert Tyler of Hartford, the Reserve rolled into a field between the Taneytown Road and the Baltimore Pike, close to the center of the Union position. Here Tyler could dispatch quickly cannon and ammunition to any section of the Union line. This move reassured General Meade, who worried about his reserve artillery and ammunition supply, fearing that the drain of ammunition on 1 July would limit the effectiveness of his artillery for the rest of the battle. But Maj. Gen. Henry J. Hunt, chief of artillery for the Army of the Potomac, assured Meade that he could meet whatever demands were made upon the reserve. As Hunt phrased it, he "directed General Tyler . . . whatever also he might leave behind, to bring up every round of ammunition in his trains, and I knew he would not fail me." Hunt had learned that Tyler was indeed an efficient and dependable artilleryman. Like Hunt, Tyler had graduated from West Point, soon winning recognition as an artillery specialist. Before his transfer to the Army of the Potomac, Tyler commanded the artillery defending Washington, Alexandria, and the Potomac River.[9]

While Tyler readied the reserve, another Connecticut general pushed his troops to their physical limits as the Sixth Corps approached Gettysburg from the southeast along the Baltimore Pike. At about 8:00 P.M. on 1 July Gen. John Sedgwick learned from Meade that his corps was needed at Gettysburg as soon as possible. At that time his men were already bivouacked near Manchester, Maryland, but Sedgwick allowed only a few hours rest before rousing the men early the next morning. By 4:00 A.M. his divisions were on the march, with "Uncle John" pushing his men to maintain a steady pace. Most of the veterans kept pace, though the "rest halts" were few and rations were eaten on the move, for the morale of the corps was high and the men had great affection for their commander. By late afternoon the Sixth Corps arrived near Gettysburg, having completed a march of nearly 34 miles in 12 hours—a remarkable feat in any army. Sedgwick's arrival was critical, and one of his aides was not understating the case when he observed that "now and then well ordered marches as effectively beat an enemy as the most decisive battle could do."[10] Meade then had his entire army at hand ready to fend off whatever attacks Lee might make.

Not a Union soldier along the perimeter doubted that Lee would strike, but they didn't know where along the line would Lee direct his confident soldiers. Flushed with their success of 1 July, the Southern rank and file believed that they would resume a direct attack on the Union lines, completing the work unfinished the day before. Lee's officers seemed equally optimistic, except for one, Lt. Gen. James Longstreet. Much has already been written about Longstreet's reluctance to order the attack against Meade's position on Cemetery Ridge on 2 July and 3 July. Longstreet tried at least twice to dissuade Lee, stressing that any attempt to storm Cemetery Ridge invited disaster, instead, urging Lee to make a grand flanking movement, sliding to the south and then to the east of Big Round Top flanking Meade's army at its southern extremity. Then the Southerners could position themselves between Meade's army and Baltimore and Washington. They might then find a relatively strong defensive position, draw Meade down from the heights at Gettysburg, and force him to attack Lee on ground more favorable to the Army of Northern Virginia. But Lee did not want to take that risk. He had no sure knowledge of Northern forces, for he had not regained the services of Stuart's cavalry, who could have probed to the south and east to check on the disposition of Union troops. Lee was sure, however, that much of the strength of Meade's army was in front of him. Lee silenced Longstreet's arguments with the response: "The enemy is there and I am going to fight him there."[11]

Reluctantly, Longstreet prepared to carry out his orders. Lee hoped to collapse both flanks of the Union line by driving two divisions of Longstreet's corps against Meade's left flank in the vicinity of Little Round Top. At the same time General Ewell's Second Corps would storm the eastern slopes of Cemetery Hill and Culp's Hill, while Hill's Third Corps would occupy the middle ground between Longstreet and Ewell, ready to assist either if needed.[12] By noon on 2 July, Longstreet had two divisions of his command moving south behind the protection of woods along Seminary Ridge, about a mile west of Cemetery Ridge. When in position, one division, under the command of Maj. Gen. John B. Hood, would point eastward through a wooded area toward Little Round Top. His second division, under Maj. Gen. Lafayette McLaws, and also hidden by woods just west of the Emmitsburg Road, would reach northward to join ranks with A. P. Hill's Third Corps. Finally Ewell's Second Corps would continue the line east through town and then turn to the southeast to encircle Cemetery Hill and Culp's Hill near Rock Creek. This was Lee's plan, and he hoped all troops would be ready to attack by early afternoon. However, thousands of Longstreet's men had to be moved unobtrusively over ground that had not been well scouted. Some counter marching was necessary for the Confederates to remain unobserved, and it was getting on toward middle afternoon before an impatient Lee received word that Longstreet was finally ready to attack.[13]

The Confederate battle line now extended some seven miles around the semicircle protected by Federal troops. Because he held the exterior line, Lee's efforts to reinforce a position or to communicate with commanders on either his left or right flank were much more difficult and time consuming. These were important considerations in an era when messages were relayed by aides on horseback. However, Lee still had confidence in his strong Southern war machine.

While Longstreet and his men were feeling their way south through the wooded terrain of Seminary Ridge, Daniel Sickles, increasingly uncomfortable with his designated position along Cemetery Ridge, considered advancing his entire Third Corps westward to the vicinity of a peach orchard bordering the Emmitsburg Road. The fact that Major General Sickles was not a military man by profession—rather, a political appointee—did not hinder him from questioning the orders that placed his corps on ground lower than the terrain about a half-mile to his front. Convinced that higher ground near the Emmitsburg Road was more suitable, he requested permission to advance. When his request was denied, Sickles, ever sure of his own judgment, moved out anyway. Using the Peach Orchard as a hinge, he swung his First Division under Maj. Gen. David Birney to the left so that its regiments stretched from the orchard to the rocky terrain of Devil's Den. The Second Division of the corps, commanded by Brig. Gen. Andrew Humphreys, prepared to defend a line running north along the Emmitsburg Road from the orchard to the Codori farmhouse. In so locating his two divisions with their accompanying artillery, Sickles created an angle at the orchard that would be most difficult to defend.[14]

One of the men attached to Humphrey's division was Joseph Hopkins Twichell, chaplain of the 71st New York. A native of Southington and a graduate of the class of 1859 at Yale, Twichell had spent the morning visiting friends on Cemetery Ridge, including Edward Carrington, a classmate at Yale now serving on the staff of Gen. John Newton of the First Corps. Returning to his unit, he found it had already begun to advance, but he caught up in time to watch Sickles's entire line advance, which he described in a letter to his sister three days later:

> Following, I overtook it formed in line of battle with the rest of the Brigade preparing to go forward. After a look and a little talk, the bugles sounded, and with a firm step with colors flying, the bravest men in the Army, marched into the open field. It was a splendid sight. For to the right and left the dark lines of infantry moved on, with the artillery disposed at intervals, while the stillness was unbroken save by the scattered fire of skirmishers in the front. My eyes and heart followed the flag which I love best and I stood unsuspicious of danger, but full of anxiety.

Sickles's troops were hardly in place before Longstreet opened his attack with an artillery barrage. Chaplain Twichell was caught by surprise, for, in his words, "the first shell struck not more than two rods behind where I with several other non-combatants were standing, expecting to see it begin from the front." Twichell and the others sought shelter at the barn belonging to Abraham Trostle, where they waited it out.

> It was awful. For half an hour it raged incessantly. Grape, Canister, solid shot and shell, whizzed and shrieked and tore past us. The trees near by were torn and dismembered. . . . Every moment I expected to be struck, but at length perceiving that our soldiers had advanced further up the field, the fire was diverted from

that point and we were released. I never experienced a deeper sense of deliverance.[15]

Following this barrage, Longstreet opened his attack and his men stormed forward, smashing into General Birney's brigades strung out along the Wheat Field and across the rugged terrain at the foot of Little Round Top. As the Rebel attack developed, Longstreet drove brigade after brigade in an en echelon movement against Sickles's defenses hinged at the Peach Orchard. The Union troops fought stubbornly, but the weight of Longstreet's attack slowly forced Birney's line south of the Wheat Field into retreat, while Humphreys's troops tried desperately to hold along the Emmitsburg Road. Along the entire line of the Third Corps, the hell of combat increased, and the rear quickly became one vast hospital. Chaplain Twichell noted that "the wounded were everywhere, and scenes of sickening horror were presented on every side." Among those badly wounded was General Sickles, who was taken behind the lines and had to have one of his legs amputated.[16]

General Meade, dismayed at Sickles's new position, recognized the threat to the Third Corps and called for reinforcements. Fortunately for him, General Sykes's Fifth Corps had reached Gettysburg earlier and was in position as a ready reserve. First to be ordered forward were the men of the First Division led by Brig. Gen. James Barnes. Two brigades of these veterans reinforced Sickles, but a third, commanded by Col. Strong Vincent, never reached the Wheat Field. Their battle stage was a hilltop. Already Southern tentacles reaching eastward toward Little Round Top wound steadily through a wooded area toward Devil's Den, close to Little Round Top.

Luckily, Meade had sent Gen. G. K. Warren to check on the defensive strength of the Round Tops. When Warren reached the summit of Little Round Top, he found to his dismay no one there but a small signal corps detachment. Recognizing that if he could not find and guide reinforcements immediately to Little Round Top Hood's brigades would soon swarm over the hill, Warren headed down the opposite side of the hill toward the Taneytown Road. By chance, General Sykes already had his troops on the move, and when Warren reached the Taneytown Road he ran into Colonel Vincent, who recognized Warren as one of General Meade's trusted officers. Directed by Warren, Vincent turned his command toward Little Round Top and sent them up the hill at double time. Somehow the artillerymen of Lt. Charles E. Hazlitt's battery also managed to drag two cannons to the top. Once there, they opened fire immediately, for Hood's Confederates were already scrambling up the other side of the hill.[17]

Within minutes this fight for Little Round Top flared into a vicious encounter. Vincent's men, now aided by Brig. Gen. Stephen H. Weed's brigade, sped their bullets toward the Rebels as fast as they could load and reload. Yet with the arrival of Hood's veterans, victory seemed almost the South's, for the Federals were fast running out of ammunition. On the extreme left of the improvised Northern line, the 20th Maine Regiment, led by Col. Joshua L. Chamberlain, was the first to exhaust its supply of bullets. Chamberlain quickly ordered his men to rely on the only thing left—cold steel. With fixed bayonets, approximately 150 men charged down the hill toward the advancing Rebels less than 200 feet away. The sheer surprise of the attack unnerved the Southerners, and they fell back in disarray.[18]

This charge by a handful of soldiers turned a hotly contested fight into gradual victory. More Northern reserves moved in, and with Little Round Top secure Meade could now concentrate on salvaging what remained of Sickles's Third Corps, heavily engaged in the Wheat Field and Peach Orchard west of Little Round Top. Gen. James Barnes, leading the First Division of the Fifth Corps, hustled his command toward the Wheat Field. Composing only two brigades now that Vincent was detached, the remaining men, commanded by Cols. William S. Tilton and Jacob B. Sweitzer, moved to the support of Col. Philip De Trobriand's Third Brigade of Birney's division, for his thin line of defense along the ravine at the southern edge of the Wheat Field had slowly given way. Their advance halted the Confederate attack momentarily, but when Gen. Lafayette MacLaws applied more pressure in a flanking movement at the western edge of the Wheat Field General Barnes decided to withdraw his men, exposing the remainder of the Northern line to a flank attack on the right. De Trobriand's brigade and his few remaining supports, then, had no choice but to retreat again, firing as they retired. Again the Southerners pushed through the lower reaches of that hard-fought ground.[19]

Pressure then came from the southwestern corner of the Wheat Field as Brig. Gen. Joseph B. Kershaw unleashed his South Carolina brigade. His objective was to silence Union artillery to the rear of the Peach Orchard and to occupy a wooded elevation, a stony hill, bordering the western edge of the Wheat Field. Supporting Kershaw's right were the Georgia regiments of Brig. Gen. Paul J. Semmes. Kershaw later reported that he

> fell back to the Third Regiment, then hotly engaged on the crest of the stony hill, and gradually swung around its right as the enemy made progress around our flank. Semmes' advanced regiment had given way. One of his regiments mingled with the Third, and, among the rocks and trees, within a few feet of each other, a desperate conflict ensued. The enemy could make no progress in front but slowly extended around my right. . . . I feared the brave men about me would be surrounded by the large force pressing around them, and ordered . . . them to fall back . . . [20]

Among the Federal forces pressing so strongly upon Kershaw and Semmes was Col. John R. Brooke's Fourth Brigade, assigned to Brig. Gen. John C. Caldwell's First Division of the Second Corps. In the middle of those Northern regiments surging forward once more were the Nutmeggers of the 27th Connecticut—all 75 of them. Commanded by Lt. Col. Henry C. Merwin, the 27th was reduced to just three small companies, for only the D and F companies escaped capture when Jackson collapsed Hooker's right flank at Chancellorsville. These companies had been detached for other duty, and, after the battle, a third company was formed from the few soldiers of the other companies not then with their units because of hospitalization or special duty. Capt. Jedediah Chapman of New Haven took command of the new company while Capt. Joseph Bradley of East Haven continued to lead Company F and Capt. Samuel T. Birdsall of New Haven commanded Company D. When these three companies lined up with the other regiments of Brooke's brigade, their banner marked the smallest fighting unit in the entire Army of the Potomac.[21]

Before Caldwell moved forward from his previous position along Cemetery Ridge he had stationed his brigades to the left of General Gibbon's Second Division, just south of the famous "little clump of trees." Brooke's Fourth Brigade nestled slightly to the rear of Gibbon's left flank. To Brooke's left, Caldwell stationed Col. Patrick Kelly's Second Brigade, known to the entire army as the Irish Brigade. The First Brigade, commanded by Col. Edward Cross, covered the left flank of the Irish Brigade, and Brig. Gen. Samuel K. Zook positioned his Third Brigade troops in rear of Kelly's brigade as a reserve for the entire First Division.[22]

When Sickles took it upon himself to move the Third Corps forward, he exposed the left flank of Caldwell's First Division of the Second Corps. Union officers and men along Cemetery Ridge were amazed by Sickles's thrust toward the Peach Orchard. General Hancock sensed disaster and immediately took measures to buttress the exposed position of the Third Corps. Lieutenant Haskell noted that "the Second Corps took arms, and the 1st Division of this Corps was ordered to be in readiness to support the Third Corps, should circumstances render support necessary."[23]

The support given Sickles by Sweitzer and Tilton helped absorb the bludgeoning of De Trobriand's thin line, but the pressure by Longstreet's men soon forced Hancock to send more Union troops forward. Caldwell's turn to stem the Rebel tide came as he pushed his division down Cemetery Ridge in a southwesterly direction, his brigades peeling off in order from the left. Colonel Cross's First Brigade led the column, followed by Kelly's Irish Brigade, then came Brooke's Fourth Brigade with the Third Brigade of General Zook bringing up the rear.

Caldwell drove his men toward the Wheat Field moving "a portion of the time at double-quick." He noted that "the position assigned me was on the right of the Fifth Corps and the left of the Third Corps, and I was ordered to check and drive back the enemy who was advancing at that point." The two brigades of General Sykes's Fifth Corps already thrown into this blood bath were now attempting to regroup at the left of the field when Caldwell arrived with his supporting division. He quickly moved to plug the gaping hole in the Union line across the Wheat Field as Longstreet's infantry again advanced. Establishing his line of attack, Caldwell fanned out his brigades behind a series of walls along the northern edge of the field. As the First Brigade approached the field, Caldwell committed it immediately and ordered Colonel Cross "to advance in line of battle through a wheat field, his left resting on the woods which skirted the field. He had advanced but a short distance when he encountered the enemy, and opened upon him a terrific fire."[24] What had been a furious struggle for these acres then became a melee as Caldwell's brigades slammed into the determined advance of the Southerners still working their way toward the northern fringe of the clearing.

Caldwell lost no time in thrusting his other brigades into action. He reported that he shoved the Irish Brigade in at the right of the First Brigade, "and they advanced in like manner, driving the enemy before them." Then came Zook's brigade, ordered by Caldwell "still farther to the right, to connect with the Third Corps."[25] Thus within minutes of his arrival Caldwell had the First, Second, and Third brigades of his division fully deployed. As these veterans closed in on the Rebels, they rifled, clubbed, and bayoneted their way toward the southern edge of the clearing.

Colonel Brooke reported that when he led his Fourth Brigade toward the Wheat Field, he followed the Irish Brigade, formed his regiments in battle line, and moved forward in supporting distance of that brigade. Then Caldwell ap-

proached and ordered Brooke to halt his advance. Next, said
Brooke, "Caldwell moved the Irish Brigade to the right, leaving my brigade in rear of and at supporting distance from the
First Brigade, which was then hotly engaged beyond the crest,
behind which I then was. In a short time the general commanding directed me to relieve the First Brigade."[26]

The stage was set for Brooke to advance through the center
of the Wheat Field and try to clear it again. The field rises
gently from its northern fringe for about 200 yards to a crest
and then slants down in a southwesterly direction towards a
low, wet area along its southern edge. Through these wetlands runs a stream heading toward Devil's Den and Plum
Run. Beyond the stream the ground rises sharply in a series of
scrub-covered rocky ledges. Just a few minutes before
Brooke's attack, the Confederates of Semmes's brigade had
scrambled down those ledges and through the wetland to support Kershaw's brigade, which was battered by the Northern
brigades of Zook and Kelly.[27] When Brooke thrust his men
forward, his five regiments formed for the charge in the following order: the 2d Delaware on the left and to their right
the men of the 64th New York, then the 53d Pennsylvania,
the 27th Connecticut, and, finally, the 145th Pennsylvania.
These regiments advanced into the Wheat Field.

Lt. Col. Henry C. Merwin, commanding the 27th Connecticut, led his thin line from the relative protection of
stone walls north of the field toward the slight crest of ground
directly ahead of him. Merwin had learned to soldier early in
the war. In 1861, he was a sergeant in the elite New Haven
Grays, one of the first companies in Connecticut to offer its
services to the federal government. Caught in the debacle of
First Bull Run as part of Col. Alfred Terry's 2d Connecticut,
Merwin survived and returned to New Haven at the end of
his 90-day enlistment. After spending a few months in business with his father and brother, he again entered service
and raised a quota of men to form Company A of the 27th
Regiment. When that unit mustered for service in October
1862, his fellow officers chose him as lieutenant colonel. At
Chancellorsville Col. Richard Bostwick, commander of the
27th, was captured along with Lieutenant Merwin and eight

companies of the regiment. Exchanged before the battle of Gettysburg, Merwin returned to lead what remained of the unit. Alert and quick to seize the initiative in military contact, he earned "respect, confidence and affection among the men in his command."[28]

As Merwin charged with his men, a Rebel bullet took him to the ground. He is reported to have whispered this final observation: "My poor regiment is suffering fearfully."[29] Command of the unit now fell upon Maj. James H. Coburn, another former member of the New Haven Grays. As he pressed the Nutmeggers forward, his right flank was supported by the 145th Pennsylvania. Capt. John C. Hilton of that regiment reported that as the attack began, a few rounds were fired. Then the 145th Pennsylvania with the 27th Connecticut on its left "moved to the center of the wheat-field, and lying down, several volleys of buck and ball were poured into Kershaw's Brigade." Then the order was given to charge. The gray-coats would not stand in front of the bayonets of the Second Corps veterans, but retreated through the Wheat Field and meadow beyond, up the ravine, and into the hornet's nest of rocks and underbrush where they halted and sent a deadly fire of lead into the Union ranks before they were dislodged.[30]

Major Coburn and his men matched the efforts of the 145th Pennsylvania. With clubbed rifles and bayonets, they drove the Rebels before them into the wetlands at the southern edge of the field. But Capt. Jedediah Chapman never made it. Near the southwest corner of the meadow he was killed by a Rebel bullet. What remained of the command still charged. Flanked by remnants of other regiments in their brigade, these Connecticut Yankees "pressed forward at double-quick, through the wheatfield and woods beyond, driving the rebels a quarter of a mile, across a ravine, which on the further side rises into a precipitous ledge."[31] When Semmes's brigade pulled back from the Wheat Field and scrambled back up the ledges beyond the wetlands, they left their commander on the field, for Semmes had fallen as he led his brigade forward to support Kershaw's right flank.

The Georgians managed to regroup atop and slightly to the rear of the ledge. As they sought to establish a defensive line there, the Connecticut contingent

> with much difficulty clambered up the rocky steep, but as they appeared upon the crest of the hill, the enemy, drawn up in readiness just beyond, within pistol-range, opened upon them a withering fire. The contest at this point continued for some time. Planting the colors upon the top, the men loaded their pieces under shelter of the brow of the hill, then, rising up, delivered their fire.[32]

The other units of Brooke's brigade kept pace with the 27th Connecticut, but it was impossible to move up and beyond the protection of the ridge.

When the Yankee attack stalled, the regiments of the brigade lined up in the same positions that marked their sweep through the Wheat Field.[33] Once Brooke's brigade had secured this ridge, their furious counterattack against the Southerners had carried them well beyond support on either flank. This indeed was a gallant charge, but all it bought was a half-hour's time for Meade to rush more reenforcements far to the rear of Brooke's advanced position—done so at great cost. In the words of Pvt. Almond E. Clark of Company C: "Our number by this time was reduced to less than half that started in the fray but we had the flags with us."[34]

Coburn's veterans and the other Federals of the brigade used the protection of the ridge to load their rifles. Then rising just enough to prop their guns on the rocks, they drew a bead and fired quickly. While his brigade sent a hail of bullets into the woods beyond the ridge where the Georgians were regrouping, Colonel Brooke urgently sought assistance, for he knew that his flanks were threatened. He reported that General Anderson's Georgia brigade was coming in on his left. Brooke noted that he "held them at bay for some time, when word was brought to me that my right was being turned, and finding no troops coming to my support . . . I reluctantly gave the order to retire."[35] Private Clark wrote, "After being there

a short time and constantly under the rebel fire we were surprised by a rebel force on our left which poured a volley into
us at short range. That was our order to fall back which we
did following the flags being all the time under the rebel fire."
As Major Coburn withdrew the 27th Connecticut, his command reached the shelter of the walls to the north of the
Wheat Field—the same walls from which, a short time before, they had charged so gallantly. Brooke withdrew his brigade just in time to prevent the capture of his command.
Longstreet had finally sent in two fresh brigades led by
Generals Barksdale and Wofford. Kershaw also managed to
get some of his regiments moving forward again. The combined strength of this last Southern charge cleared both the
Peach Orchard and the Wheat Field of effective Northern
opposition.

As the decimated regiments of the Fourth Brigade tried to
sort themselves out they were ready, said Brooke, "to fight to
the last." Fortunately, they were soon relieved by troops from
the Twelfth Corps. Hancock then ordered Caldwell to march
his First Division "back to the ground it had occupied in the
earlier part of the day." There the 27th Connecticut, reduced
to 37 men, bivouacked for the night.[36]

When the haze and smoke of battle lifted toward sunset,
Longstreet's Southerners controlled the lower reaches of
Devil's Den, the Wheat Field, and the Peach Orchard. But he
had paid a terrible price in casualties for a few acres of land,
and two of his three divisions would not be ready for battle on
the following day. Lee had not planned it that way. There was
much discomfort in the Southern camp that night.

When Caldwell's division retreated to Cemetery Ridge, its
position was near the ground it had previously occupied.
There his exhausted troops lay on their arms until ordered to
reform along the ridge early in the morning of 3 July. By
chance this placed the 27th Connecticut and the four other
regiments of Brooke's brigade in the immediate vicinity of
Capt. John W. Sterling's 2d Connecticut Light Battery. Once
positioned there the 27th became "busily engaged in throwing up entrenchments, gathering for this purpose rails and
stones from neighboring fences, and in the absence of picks

and shovels, using their bayonets and tin plates to heap up the earth."[37]

The area in the brigade line assigned to the Connecticut Yankees must have been small indeed, for the command had lost half its fighting strength on 2 July. Along with Lieutenant Colonel Merwin and Captain Chapman, nine others were killed or missing, and 27 wounded. Their sacrifices did not go unnoticed. Colonel Brooke called General Hancock's attention to "the little remnant of the 27th, alluding, in strong terms of commendation, to the conduct of the regiment in the action of the preceding afternoon." Hancock congratulated the men for their valor, encouraging them to "Stand well to your duty now, and in a few days you will carry with you to your homes all the honors of this, the greatest battle ever fought upon the continent."[38]

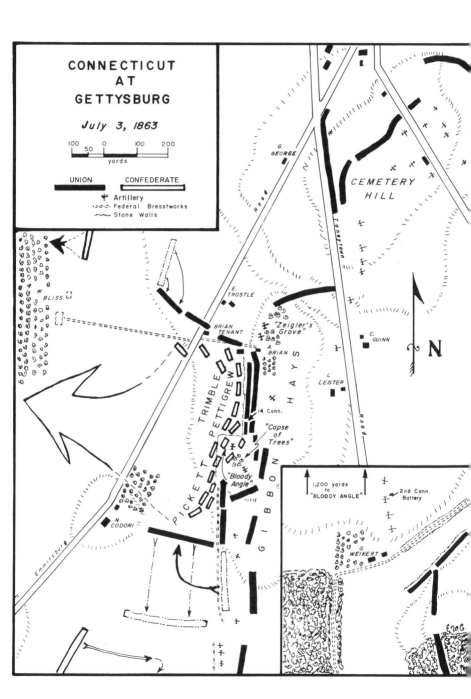

# CONNECTICUT
## AT
## GETTYSBURG

### July 3, 1863

100    0    100    200
50
yards

UNION    CONFEDERATE

† Artillery
Federal Breastworks
Stone Walls

G. GEORGE

CEMETERY
HILL

N

Road

Taneytown

E. TROSTLE

"Zeigler's Grove"

BRIAN TENANT

A. BRIAN

C. GUINN

14 Conn.

H A Y S

L LEISTER

W BLISS

"Copse of Trees"

"Bloody Angle"

Road

P I C K E T T    T R I M B L E    P E T T I G R E W

N CODORI

G I B B O N

Emmitsburg

1,200 yards to "BLOODY ANGLE"

2nd Conn. Battery

G. WEIKERT

E. 2o.G.

# "We Had a Hand-to-Hand Conflict" 4 The 17th Connecticut at East Cemetery Hill

His lips went back. He felt something swell in his
 chest
Like a huge, indocile bubble. "By God," he said,
Loading and firing, "You're not going to get this hill,
You're not going to get this hill. By God, but you're
 not."
—Stephen Vincent Benét, *John Brown's Body*

TOWARD SUNSET on 2 July, when Maj. James Coburn withdrew what remained of his 27th Connecticut from the Wheat Field, he ordered his exhausted Yankees to bed down on the western slope of Cemetery Ridge. For these battered veterans, the day's combat was over. But across the hill on the eastern side of the ridge, the story was altogether different. Maj. Allen Brady, commander of the 17th Connecticut, realized that for his men a fight was about to begin.

At eventide Brady had posted his infantry along the walls of a lane running across the eastern face of Cemetery Hill, about 200 feet below its summit. On a small plateau atop the hill, Col. Charles S. Wainwright, commanding the Artillery Brigade of the First Corps, had in position several Union batteries with muzzles pointing east.[1] Below these guns, and about halfway down a steep decline, Brady's Yankees hastily dug in along the lane. Let us review the movements that brought them to this point.

The position of Brady's men at this time was dictated by events of the day before, for when the Southerners cleared

General Barlow's division from the knoll northeast of Gettysburg in the late afternoon of 1 July, they drove the Federals toward the center of town. Under Major Brady's command, the men of the 17th Connecticut fought their way through town to the sanctuary of Cemetery Hill. Here they redeployed under the direct supervision of General Howard, for the moment commander of Federal forces at Gettysburg. Major Brady reported that after a tour of picket duty, his men returned to their former position on the north face of Cemetery Hill looking toward town.[2] By that time, 2:00 A.M. on 2 July, General Ames had reassembled the remnants of his broken division. Under Howard's orders, he anchored the left of his defensive line on the Baltimore Pike facing north toward Gettysburg and extended the line easterly along a rail fence that dipped downhill to reach a lane running at right angles to the fence (the lane is now called Wainwright Avenue).

When Brady returned from picket duty with his men, he found his original position on the northern face of the hill manned by the 107th Ohio, its left flank hard against the Baltimore Pike. To the right of the 107th, Col. Andrew L. Harris, commanding the Second Brigade, had posted the 25th Ohio. Brady took position on the right flank of the 25th Ohio, "150 paces to the right of the place we occupied before going out on picket." Here his regiment remained, exposed to intermittent fire from Southern sharpshooters until 7:00 P.M. Brady's veterans were then ordered to pull out of their position and reform "behind a stone wall on each side of a lane below the battery opposite the cemetery entrance."[3]

Brady's men prepared their defense against the same Rebels that had driven them through the streets of Gettysburg on the previous afternoon—and these Confederates were at nearly full strength. When General Gordon captured Barlow's Knoll on the afternoon of 1 July, his left flank was protected by Gen. Harry Hays's Louisiana Tigers and Gen. Robert Hoke's North Carolina brigade, now commanded by Col. Isaac Avery. Both brigades swept into Gettysburg with very few casualties, for it was Gordon who carried much of the battle. And Gordon's Georgians were responsible for most of the casualties that thinned the ranks of the 17th Connecticut. The Nutmeggers lost 38 percent of their effective strength that afternoon, and on 2 July faced another Rebel surge with but 241 of their men behind the wall and very little infantry strength on either flank. Major Brady did not have much time to gather in supports, but he claimed that "we covered the wall on each side of the lane by compelling about 300 stragglers who had no commander to fall into our line."[4] Brady's caustic tongue and the flat of his sabre must have been very persuasive, for Civil War stragglers were most reluctant to face the enemy with any regiments but their own.

Once Brady extended his line, he positioned it to connect with the left regiment of Col. Leopold von Gilsa's First Brigade. These were the troops that were the first to break at Barlow's Knoll on the preceding day, creating additional confusion as they scattered in retreat through the ranks of adjacent regiments. Battered physically as well as in reputation, von Gilsa's remaining soldiers were positioned along the southern extension of the lane on Brady's right flank; on his immediate right, von Gilsa had in position what remained of the 54th and 68th New York.[5]

When Colonel Harris ordered Brady to withdraw the 17th Connecticut from the Second Brigade line facing north, he knew that his regiments would come under attack from the east. Southern artillery had already fired upon the eastern front of Cemetery Hill, and three brigades of Southern infantry were moving toward the fields and wooded areas that lay to the east of the hill. To meet this thrust, Harris readjusted his lines by facing the 17th Connecticut east behind the walls along the lane. Now the 75th Ohio buttressed Connecticut's left flank.[6] This shift in position meant that only two Ohio regiments, the 107th and the 25th, were left to protect the northern approach to Cemetery Hill near the Baltimore Pike.

Gen. Jubal Early assigned three brigades to the attack on Cemetery Hill; this time Gordon's brigade served as a reserve while Hays and Avery led their troops in the assault. Lee's timetable called for the attack to coincide with Longstreet's thrust against Meade's left flank. Somehow General Ewell failed to grasp the intent of the plan. Lee expected that his First and Second corps would strike the Federal flanks

simultaneously, making it doubly difficult for Meade to deploy his reserve. But Longstreet's attack against Meade's left
had lost its momentum before Ewell turned his men loose
about 7:00 P.M. Consequently, Union commanders were able
to concentrate on repelling Longstreet before turning their attention to Ewell's late onslaught.[7]

The Union line along the northern and eastern rim of
Cemetery Hill was thin, but Howard and Hancock had
strengthened that area with several batteries of artillery.
When Hays and Avery moved their two brigades—almost at
full strength—into position for attack, they would fight two
Federal brigades able to field less then two-thirds of their original strength. The regiments of Colonels Harris and von
Gilsa were positioned along the sides of the hill. Harris's
command began with the left of the line, with the 107th and
25th Ohio facing north and the 75th Ohio and 17th Connecticut facing east. Joining this brigade was the left of von Gilsa's
brigade, the 54th and 68th New York, facing southeast, and
the three remaining regiments were in position facing east behind a stone wall at the base of the hill.[8]

Fortunately for the North, von Steinwehr, commanding
Howard's Second Division, and Colonel Wainwright, artillery
commander of the First Corps, had posted several batteries in
strategic positions on a plateau above the infantry. Any infantry assaulting the north, east, or southeast side of Cemetery
Hill were subjected to heavy cannon fire long before they
reached the foot of the hill. However, because of the steep decline of the eastern side of the hill, guns firing from that direction lost control of their immediate front once enemy
troops reached the bottom of the hill, for the guns could not
be depressed to a degree where they might hit the assaulting
columns. While making his rounds, General Hancock noticed this weakness and ordered another battery placed on a
small knoll about 400 yards southeast of Cemetery Hill.
From this position the guns of the battery were trained upon
enemy infantry approaching through the farmlands to the
north, "and by swinging the trails sharp to the right, the
steep acclivities of East Cemetery Hill were within canister
range. The fields at the foot of the hill, inaccessible to the

guns on the crest, could be swept clean of any troops assailing our front at that point by an enfilading fire of double canister."[9] The six 12-pound cannons rolled into position on the small knoll between East Cemetery Hill and Culp's Hill were manned by 5th Maine artillerymen. Von Steinwehr also strengthened that area with another infantry regiment. Col. Adin B. Underwood hustled his 33d Massachusetts Regiment into line behind a stone wall at the foot of the hill. Here they faced northeast, their right flank under the guns of the 5th Maine Artillery and their left flank reaching out toward von Gilsa's regiments at the base of Cemetery Hill.

Late in the afternoon of 2 July, Ewell shook the Union troops on Cemetery Hill with several rounds of artillery fire from cannons on Benner's Hill, a rise of ground less than a mile northeast of Cemetery Hill. Concentrated artillery fire from Cemetery Hill soon drove the Rebel cannoneers down the other side of Benner's Hill, but the alarm had been sounded. Ewell was testing Union artillery strength before launching an infantry attack. He seems to have been reluctant to drive Early's troops forward until Maj. Gen. Edward Johnson's Confederate division had moved against Culp's Hill on Early's left flank.[10]

As the sun began to slide down behind Cemetery Hill, the head of the Confederate column emerged from the southeast corner of Gettysburg. During the afternoon the brigades of General Hays and Colonel Avery had occupied a field "between the city and the base of a hill intervening between us and Cemetery Hill." Hays wrote that he was ordered at that time by Early "to hold my brigade in readiness at a given signal to charge the enemy in the works on the summit of the hill before me, with the information that a general advance of our entire line would be made at the same time."[11] But it was almost 8:00 P.M. before General Hays received orders to move his men. North Carolina led the column and Louisiana followed. General Gordon's Georgia brigade moved into the area vacated by General Hays, ready as a reserve if needed. As the column entered the fields beyond the edge of town, the Confederates moved in a southeasterly direction until the rear element of the Louisiana Tigers cleared the town. Then both brigades deployed into line, turned to the right, and moved directly toward the eastern slopes of Cemetery Hill.

Behind the walls on the eastern face of Cemetery Hill, Brady steadied his Connecticut troops. He had taken position along that front just a few minutes before. When Hays wheeled to the right and ordered the assault on the hill, his attack centered upon the point protected by the 17th Connecticut. As soon as Brady's Yankees settled in behind the walls, "two companies were advanced to the grain field near the woods through which the enemy were rapidly advancing." These woods were below Brady's left flank, and the Louisiana Tigers on the right of the Rebel line were seeking what shelter the scrub and trees afforded. As soon as the head of the Rebel column appeared from the corner of town, it faced the cannons of the 5th Maine. The Confederates were already in range of these guns, "and as quickly as the enemy appeared, even while his lines were forming, the battery opened with spherical case, each one bursting as if on measured ground, at the right time and in the right place in front of their formation."[12]

The Confederates were not the only ones caught in the Union artillery fire. Lt. Milton Daniels of Company C, 17th Connecticut, had led his men forward along with Company D to act as skirmishers on the unit's left flank. He noted later that "the battery in our rear was giving them [the Confederates] a warm reception with grape and canister, firing over our heads. I remember the lead wadding from one shot killed one of our men, which demoralized us worse than the enemy in front."[13]

The bombardment dropped on the Confederate lines by the 5th Maine alerted all the batteries along Cemetery Hill; 16 more guns soon opened fire. This complicated General Ewell's plans, for he had made no arrangements for artillery support. The Louisiana Tigers and North Carolinians were all alone in their attempt to force their way into and through the Northern lines. It was slow, deadly work across some 600 yards of rolling farmland cut up by stone walls. As the Southerners advanced, they sought whatever cover the terrain afforded, loaded and fired, and then moved on again. Such tactics tended to undo whatever alignment the regiments had as they wheeled into position for the charge, but their determination carried them forward.[14]

Major Brady recalled his two companies of skirmishers as the Confederate attack came in close. He noted that "the enemy were discovered advancing rapidly upon us on our right and a full brigade obliquely on our left. When within 150 paces of us, we poured a destructive fire upon them, which thinned their ranks and checked their advance."[15] While this stage of the fighting was underway, Lieutenant Daniels observed two of his men who were "particularly noticeable for coolness," Privates George Woods of Danbury and William Curtis of Newtown, both of Company C.

> While the Tigers were coming across the meadow George and Bill were sitting down behind the stone wall, and you would have supposed that they were shooting at a target. I saw George shoot, taking a dead rest, and heard him say, "He won't come any further, will he, Bill?" Then Bill shot, and said: "I got that fellow, George." And they kept it up that way, perfectly oblivious to danger themselves.[16]

Coming in on Brady's right were the North Carolinians. Under Colonel Avery's command their left flank swung into a position that exposed them to a deadly enfilading fire from the guns of the 5th Maine Artillery. Sensing in the gathering gloom of the evening that his regiments were too far to the left, Colonel Avery somehow managed to wheel his brigade front toward the right. Now the men from North Carolina drove directly toward von Gilsa's regiments at the foot of Cemetery Hill, and once again von Gilsa's "Dutchmen" broke and withdrew toward the top of the hill. Colonel Avery was fatally wounded at this time, but his regiments pushed forward. Suddenly another obstacle appeared in their path: the 17th Connecticut had moved laterally to their own right to plug the gap created by von Gilsa's retreat.[17]

Major Brady had trouble enough before his right flank became exposed, for until that time his men and the 75th Ohio had been fighting off the Louisiana Tigers coming in on the Union left. Behind Connecticut's position, the slope of Cemetery Hill rose abruptly, and directly overhead the guns of Wiedrich's Battery L, 1st New York Light Artillery, ceased firing, for his cannon could not be depressed low enough to fire upon the Southerners. Hays and his Louisiana Tigers surged forward, attempting to reach the walls protected by Connecticut and Ohio. As they charged from the bottom of the hill, they came under canister fire from the guns of the 5th Maine, raking the entire Southern line with deadly effect. As it fast grew dark, the smoke and dust overhanging the hillside created an eerie setting for climax of the day's fight.[18]

Brady's Connecticut Yankees were directly in front of the first charge of the Louisiana Tigers, and they met them head on. Brady noted: "We fired several volleys by battalion, after which they charged us. We had a hand-to-hand conflict with them, firmly held our ground, and drove them back."[19] But the Tigers lost little time in regrouping for another try; they were then supported on their left by a North Carolina regiment. Caught in a hail of canister from the 5th Maine Artillery, Avery's Confederates crowded to the right. Still pushing forward, these Southerners soon clashed with von Gilsa's regiments in their immediate front. However, the 6th North Carolina on the right of Avery's brigade found itself clustering with General Hays's Louisiana regiments at the foot of the hill. Undaunted by bursts of canister and intense rifle fire, these Confederates caught their second wind and surged forward again, scrambling up to the walls along the lane defended by the 17th Connecticut. But the Yankees were not behind the walls; the regiment had been ordered to the right to fill the gap created by the collapse of von Gilsa's 54th New York Regiment, for "the remnant of that regiment was pushed up the hill, close to the cemetery."[20] When Brady moved his Connecticut Yankees to the right, "Coming to the relief of the exhausted Fifty-fourth," he opened up a hole in the line that Colonel Harris had no chance to fill. The Confederates, driving for the summit came "through the opening in our lines caused by this change of position of the 17th." Once over the walls bordering the lane, the Southerners resorted to a hand-to-hand struggle. Not many Rebels reached this breach in the Northern line, but the few who succeeded fought viciously. They were strong enough to bend back the right of the 75th Ohio, break off two companies, and sweep them aside. The rest of the regiment held firm.[21]

Brady found himself in the middle of a tremendous dog-fight. He reported that with "some of the troops on our left giving way, the rebels succeeded in getting in our rear." Bayonets and clubbed rifles, sabres and stones, and brute strength—they were the weapons suited for that kind of conflict. Into this jumbled mass of fighting humanity, Northern cannoneers fired canister. Major Brady went down during the melee, "wounded by a fragment of a shell, which hit him upon the right shoulder." But his Connecticut regiment on the right of the gap managed to repulse the weakening thrusts of Avery's remaining regiments. The 21st North Carolina made a desperate attempt to clear the Nutmeggers from the hill, but they faced "a continual stream of fire," and after re-forming and charging again they were forced to withdraw.[22]

Fragments of the 6th North Carolina managed to turn the left flank and get in the rear of the 17th Connecticut as they struggled up the steep incline toward the silent artillery. The guns were their objective. General Hays also pushed some of his Louisiana Tigers through the breach in the wall, turned the right flank of the 75th Ohio, and scrambled toward the summit. The 9th Louisiana and a portion of the 6th North Carolina succeeded in fighting their way up the channel in the hill between the 75th Ohio and the 17th Connecticut. About 100 of these Southerners reached the crest, bursting in among the cannoneers protecting their artillery. Capt. Edward G. Whittier, commanding the 5th Maine Artillery, remembers that

> of all the men in the two brigades leading the Confederate assault only eight-seven found the way to the top of the crest (so reported by Major Samuel Tate, 6th North Carolina Regiment), and that these few brave men in the darkness, "traveling in the line of least resistance," stumbled upon the gap in our infantry lines

made by the moving of the 17th Connecticut to the place where von Gilsa's brigade had just demonstrated their lack of staying qualities.[23]

While the men of the 17th Connecticut and the 75th Ohio fought to close the gap in the Union line, the cannoneers at the top of the hill were compelled to slug it out with the Confederates storming their gun emplacements. The Rebels swarmed first into Wiedrich's battery and quickly cleared his gun pits. They then rushed toward Bruce Ricketts's consolidated F and G batteries of the 1st Pennsylvania Light Artillery. Here they ran into even more stubborn resistance, as the gunners resorted to using handspikes, rammers, and pistol butts to fight off the infantry. Stunned by the tenacity of Ricketts's men, the Confederates captured only one or two guns. As this handful of exhausted Rebels struggled to keep control of the guns already taken, General Hays awaited the supporting troops promised him by General Early. Hays had been told to expect support from the opposite side of the hill, but Longstreet had failed earlier in the evening to gain the heights, and Gen. Robert Rodes had decided not to move forward, although Ewell, his corps commander, had ordered him to support Hays.[24]

Obviously the Confederates were now in a precarious position. They had reached their objective, the crest of Cemetery Hill, and had captured some of the guns that had killed many of their comrades. But they were alone. Hays looked anxiously down the slope hoping to see or hear evidence that Gordon's Georgians were moving to his support, but he searched in vain. Strangely, General Gordon never moved his brigade that evening, and he could never satisfactorily explain this martial lapse in his otherwise brilliant military career.[25] And for General Hays this lapse meant disaster.

Federals were advancing quickly from the opposite side of Cemetery Hill, and this new pressure forced Hays to withdraw his valiant band to the wall facing town. He then "gave the order to retire to the stone wall at the foot of the hill. . . .

From this position I subsequently fell back to a fence some 75 yards distant from the wall, and awaited the further movement of the enemy."[26]

Meanwhile the Connecticut Yankees had been struggling to keep their immediate rear free of any Confederates. When the breakthrough occurred, most of the Rebels strained to reach the cannons along the crest. The few that may have approached Brady's left flank and rear were soon repulsed. Brady reported that "We again drove them back and held our position." The pressure of Avery's North Carolina regiments on the front of the Connecticut line was severe. But the constant shelling of Avery's Confederates—enfiladed and pelted with canister from the guns of the 5th Maine Artillery and driven by rifle fire from the 17th Connecticut—forced them to give way and crowd to their right, bunched at the foot of the hill near the point of the original breakthrough. They could not sort themselves out for a charge up the hill to help their comrades battling the Union artillerymen.[27] The Connecticut Yankees refused to be dislodged and continued to load and fire into the mass of Confederates seeking cover at the base of the hill.

When Hays tumbled back down the slope with the Confederate survivors of his charge, the fight for the summit was over. Darkness covered the surrounding terrain, and the chatter of small-arms fire diminished. Suddenly, along the crest of the hill there appeared a full brigade of Federal infantry sent to the scene by General Hancock. Although Howard's troops had by now contained and driven back the Rebel assault, Col. Samuel S. Carroll, the fiery leader of this fresh brigade, insisted on getting into the action. In the dark, at about 9:00 P.M., he spread his three regiments across the top of Cemetery Hill and sent them charging down the slope through the Federal line reestablished along the walls of the lane and into the bottom land at the foot of the hill. Colonel Wainwright, commanding the Union batteries on the hilltop, commented that he did not think "Carroll would find many live rebs there." This was indeed the case, though Carroll managed to strike the rear of the Southern retreating columns and capture some prisoners. When Colonel Carroll returned from the base of the hill, the sounds of battle again subsided. Major Brady's Connecticut Yankees, tense and still wrought-up, again spread out along the wall and closed the gap exploited by the Louisiana Tigers. Brady recalled that "after the enemy had been driven back, the firing ceased, excepting occasional shots from their sharpshooters."[28]

Although Brady had been stunned and wounded by shrapnel, he continued his command of the 17th Connecticut, penning his battle report to his superiors on 4 July 1863. The toll in dead and wounded ran high for both the North and South in this fierce encounter. The brigades of Hays and Avery drove toward East Cemetery Hill with some 2,500 men, but they lost 746—nearly 30 percent of the men engaged. The First and Second brigades of Barlow's former division numbered about 1,150 men that evening, 241 of them in the 17th Connecticut. When the fighting ceased, there were 62 Nutmegger casualties, another 26 percent of the unit's fighting strength. The 17th Connecticut had entered Gettysburg on 1 July with 17 officers and 369 men; by the morning of 3 July, it had lost its commander, seven other officers, and 190 men. Only 179 men from Connecticut left Gettysburg on 4 July 1863 with Meade's victorious army.[29]

Even though the unit's loss had been heavy, the men had gained much honor, and Maj. Allen Brady had proven himself a worthy leader. Denied regimental command throughout his military career, Brady won at Gettysburg the chance to command in battle. He brought his Connecticut regiment through two days of hard fighting, and in the final moments of the melee with the Louisiana Tigers on Cemetery Hill, Brady was knocked to the ground by a shell fragment that broke his scapula. His leadership at Gettysburg offset his previous "impetuous indiscretion," and his actions were "mostly amply atoned for by his subsequent honorable and extremely efficient service."[30]

# "Only a Battle Would Give Us Possession"

# 5

# The 5th and 20th Connecticut at Culp's Hill

The morning wears with a stubborn fight on Culp's
  Hill
That ends at last in Confederate repulse
And that barb-end of the fish-hook cleared of the grey.
        —Stephen Vincent Benét, *John Brown's Body*

MAJ. GEN. EDWARD JOHNSON's division was the last of Ewell's Second Corps to reach Gettysburg. Early in the evening of 1 July his brigades approached from the northwest, proceeded through the town, and took position on the far left of the Confederate perimeter. Johnson's troops had been selected to storm Culp's Hill at the same time that Longstreet unleashed his assault at the Round Tops.[1] Johnson spent the morning and early afternoon of 2 July pushing his brigades through the woods and fields on the far side of Rock Creek, where sluggish and muddy waters curled around the eastern footings of Culp's Hill.

At the same time, Gen. Henry W. Slocum's Twelfth Corps was busy fortifying the higher elevations of that same hill. Among the regiments engaged in throwing up breastworks were two from Connecticut, the 5th and 20th, brigaded together in the First Division of Slocum's corps. This division took its orders from another son of Connecticut, Brig. Gen. Alpheus S. Williams. A native of Saybrook, Williams graduated from Yale in 1831 and then traveled extensively in Europe before returning home to study law. He established a practice in Detroit then moved to a judgeship, before serving

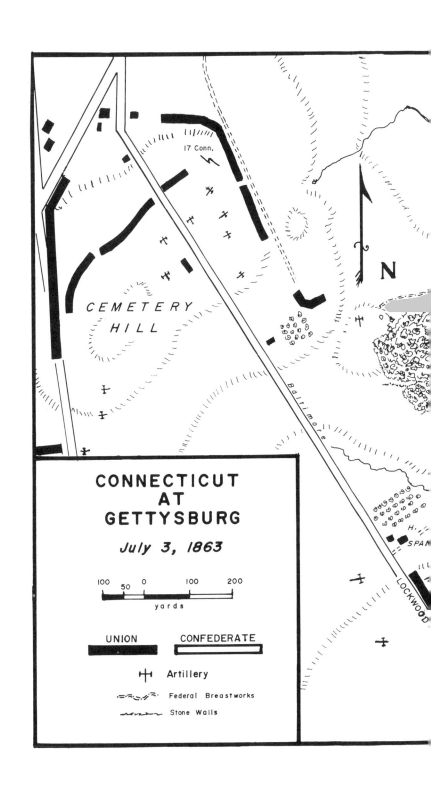

17 Conn.

N

CEMETERY
HILL

Baltimore

## CONNECTICUT
## AT
## GETTYSBURG

*July 3, 1863*

100  50  0      100      200
yards

UNION          CONFEDERATE

✛ Artillery

Federal Breastworks

Stone Walls

H.
SPAN

LOCKWOOD

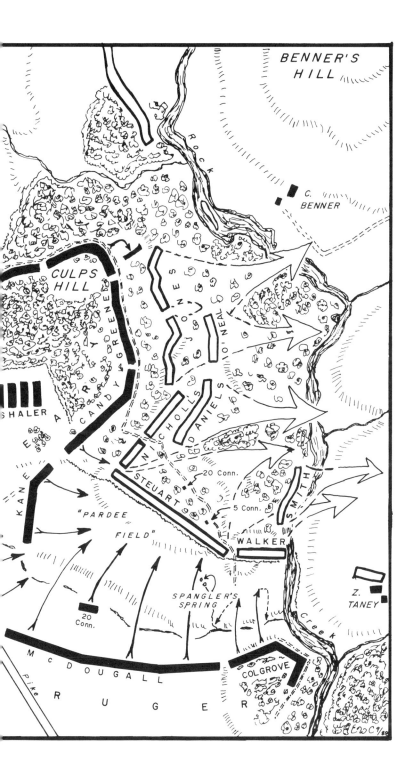

BENNER'S HILL

ROCK

C. BENNER

CULPS HILL

SHALER

GREENE

CANDY

N I C H O L L S

D A N I E L S

O'NEAL

N E S

KANE

STEUART

20 Conn.

5 Conn.

S M I T H

Z. TANEY

"PARDEE" FIELD

20 Conn.

WALKER

SPANGLER'S SPRING

Creek

McDOUGALL

R U G E R

COLGROVE

Pike

as a lieutenant colonel with the Michigan Volunteers in the Mexican War. Although he was more than 50 years old when the Civil War began, Williams lost little time in volunteering for service. Commissioned as a brigadier general in May 1861, he led a division of the Twelfth Corps in battles at South Mountain and Antietam.[2] Steady and dependable, Williams was called "Old Pap" by his troops. Later he would command the Twentieth Corps on Sherman's "March to the Sea." But at Gettysburg on 2 July, this Connecticut-born general had to secure and hold Culp's Hill.

Although Slocum seemed reluctant to take his corps into the thick of the struggle on 1 July, he did bring his divisions forward late in the afternoon. Cautious in his advance along the Baltimore Pike, he spread his brigades to the right and left of the road, extended his picket lines, and brought his corps to a standstill about two miles from Cemetery Hill. Then, at about 7:00 P.M., with a few staff officers, he rode forward to Howard's command post just outside the entrance to the cemetery. Slocum learned firsthand of the cost the veterans of the First and Eleventh corps paid to secure the heights south of Gettysburg, and he realized that his own corps was in a logical position to protect Culp's Hill, the eastern anchor of the Union line. Slocum also learned that Little Round Top was undefended, and before sunset he had his Second Division, led by Brig. Gen. John W. Geary, moving forward to occupy that hill and its adjacent terrain. There the division camped for the night.[3]

The leadership of the Twelfth Corps fell to General Williams once Slocum assumed command of the army on the field at Gettysburg. Williams continued to lead the corps for the rest of the battle, even after Meade arrived early on 2 July, for Meade designated Slocum commander of his right wing. Two of Meade's seven corps commanders at Gettysburg were natives of Connecticut: Maj. Gen. John Sedgwick of the Sixth Corps and Brig. Gen. Alpheus Williams of the Twelfth Corps.

Once in command and aware of his assignment to fortify Culp's Hill, Williams shook his troops out at dawn on 2 July and parceled each division out to the terrain it was to protect. On the march to Gettysburg, the 5th and 20th Connecticut regiments trudged toward town as part of the First Brigade of the First Division. Their brigade commander, Col. Archibald L. McDougall, counted four other regiments among his command. The 5th Connecticut mustered 221 veterans as Col. Warren W. Packer brought his regiment to a halt on the outskirts of town. Within hailing distance, the 20th Connecticut, 321 men strong, eased off the Baltimore Pike under the orders of Lt. Col. William B. Wooster.[4]

When Slocum rode forward to confer with Howard, Williams secured his command for the night. The First Division bivouacked on the right side of the pike as the Second Division tramped off to the vicinity of Little Round Top. A few First Division regiments were assigned to duty as pickets and skirmishers; the rest of the command bedded down for a few hours' sleep.

The 5th Connecticut had little if any rest during the night of 1 July. Colonel Packer reported that when within one mile of Gettysburg his regiment "filed to the right toward Culp's Hill, and after marching nearly 1 mile, formed line of battle; were then ordered to support a section of Battery M, First New York Artillery. Upon being relieved of this duty, we were thrown forward as skirmishers."[5] The 20th Connecticut escaped duty as pickets or skirmishers. Amid the turmoil of thousands seeking bivouac areas for the night, Colonel Wooster bedded his Yankees down adjacent to the other regiments of Colonel McDougall's First Brigade, in a field bordering the road just south of Culp's Hill. Wooster had earned the respect of his superior officers and the soldiers he commanded. Though stern and resolute, he cared about the welfare of his men. "In camp, upon the march, on the field of battle, while always exacting the strictest discipline, he was never unmindful of the safety and protection of his men, losing no opportunity to offer aid and comfort to those around him."[6] When the fighting erupted around Culp's Hill, Wooster vented his feelings like a biblical prophet, threatening catastrophe to Northern artillerymen carelessly dropping shells short among his Nutmeggers.

At dawn on 2 July, Colonel Packer drew in the 5th Connecticut from its position "as skirmishers 1½ miles in advance of the brigade." He reported that he had seen no enemy and rejoined his brigade at 4:00 A.M.[7]

Meanwhile General Williams learned the part his Twelfth Corps was to play in Meade's scheme for the defense of the Gettysburg hills. Ordered to occupy, fortify, and defend Culp's Hill, Williams roused his troops at dawn and assigned positions to his division commanders. He then hustled his entire command toward the lower reaches of the hill. The 5th and 20th Connecticut, along with other elements of the First Division, climbed the southern and southeastern slopes, crossed the summit, and went to work fortifying that section of Culp's Hill facing northeast and east. The hill had been occupied by the First Corps after its retreat through Gettysburg in late afternoon on 1 July. Under Maj. Gen. John Newton's command, these Connecticut veterans lost no time in securing their positions against possible attack.[8]

At 6:00 A.M. Brigadier General Geary collected the brigades of his Second Division near Little Round Top and headed back across Cemetery Ridge. As he approached Culp's Hill, Williams informed him that his division was to take position on the right flank of Wadsworth's troops, posted so that its left formed a right angle with Wadsworth's division. Consequently, the defensive line on Culp's Hill included Wadsworth's division on the left facing north, then Geary's men extended along the northeastern edges of the hill, and finally Brig. Gen. Thomas H. Ruger's brigades were facing toward the northeast and curling east and southeast, where the foot of the hill slid into Rock Creek. At this point Ruger acted as temporary commander of the First Division, Twelfth Corps, and in the area protected by this division the 5th and 20th Connecticut staked out their boundaries. Dropping their rifles, they grabbed axes, picks, and shovels and set to work fortifying their front. The entire Federal line "instinctively felt that a life and death struggle was impending, and that every help should be used. . . . Right and left the men felled trees, and blocked them up in a close log fence. Piles of cordwood which lay nearby were quickly appropriated. . . . Fortunate regiments which had spades and picks strengthened their work with earth. By 10 o'clock it was finished."[9]

The 5th and 20th Connecticut kept pace with their comrades along the line. Soon a solid front of breastworks
shielded their position left of the Second Division. "The 20th
Connecticut was in the front line on the left of the First Brigade," and the 5th Connecticut dug in about 150 feet downhill and to the right of the 20th Regiment. In a heavily
wooded area about a third of the way up the hillside, these
two regiments, along with their brigade, faced east. Through
the trees below them meandered Rock Creek, and across that
stream General Johnson was busy getting his brigades in position to attack. Already his skirmishers were feeling out
Union defenses along Culp's Hill. Maj. Philo B. Buckingham,
executive officer of the 20th Connecticut, noted that "during
the forenoon the fitful fire of skirmishers, as it pattered along
the left and center of the line, told us that the foe was vigi-
lant, and that the storm of battle might burst upon us at
any moment."[10]

The whistling and zinging of bullets through the woods of
Culp's Hill were familiar sounds to Buckingham, a native of
Seymour. At Chancellorsville one bullet removed all the hair
from his head—and for a moment the major lost his dignity
as well as his hair. While Buckingham was talking with General Williams and others,

> a bullet passed through his hat, grazed the top of his
> head, and—to the great astonishment and alarm of his
> brother officers—left the gallant Major as bald as a "hea-
> then Chinee." The hat and wig (the wearing of which
> nobody had previously suspected) were carried a consid-
> erable distance. "Are you badly hurt?" shouted General
> Williams, as the Major started at a double quick to re-
> claim his flying head gear. "Oh, no!" was the reply, "but
> my wig is. I guess I'll finish whipping out the Confed-
> eracy now, bald headed"; which he did, and continued
> also in that condition ever afterwards.[11]

But the storm of battle that Buckingham expected on
Culp's Hill never broke that afternoon. General Ewell
chose not to push his divisions toward the hilltops south of

Gettysburg. Again on 2 July Ewell seemed reluctant to attack, although General Johnson now had his men in position. At about 4:00 P.M., the defenders of Culp's Hill did hear heavy cannonading to their rear as Longstreet's men got into motion, but apart from a few bursts of cannon fire from Benner's Hill, the only noise coming from Ewell's wing was the crackle of sporadic skirmishing fire.

Ewell's failure to attack when Longstreet moved forward forced Meade to change his defensive tactics. First he moved into the battle against Longstreet those reserves close at hand. Then, since Ewell exerted no pressure on the opposite flank, Meade called for the Twelfth Corps to withdraw from its prepared defenses and ordered General Williams to march his command to the opposite flank of the Northern line. Fortunately, General Slocum, commanding the right wing of Meade's army, retained a brigade of the corps and spread its regiments behind the breastworks vacated by troops pulling out to oppose Longstreet. When Williams withdrew his men, the 5th and 20th Connecticut pulled out with them. They formed in column by brigades and stumbled out of the woods "on the double" to the Baltimore Pike. There General Williams took position at the head of his command as the First Division marched toward Cemetery Ridge. Williams had ordered his Second Division to fall in behind and follow the First Division, but somehow, in coming out of the woods, a confused leader of this division guided it in the wrong direction. "The Second Division marched down the pike to the rear." Unaware that he had lost half his command, Williams pushed on toward Cemetery Ridge. Eager to get into the conflict raging in the fields below Little Round Top, he drove his division forward "following the staff officer sent to conduct it to the left."[12]

Williams followed his guide along the Baltimore Pike for a short distance and then led his column off the shoulder of the road toward Cemetery Ridge. His route took him and his division cross-country through fields and scrubland, up and across the spine of Cemetery Ridge, and then down its western slopes just behind the Wheat Field. Along the way his brigades came under sporadic but ineffective shelling from

Longstreet's artillery. Pvt. Abner C. Smith of East Haddam, a member of Company C, wrote to his wife two days later that

> the rebs had a battery playing onto us all the way from where we started till we got where it was thought we should be needed. One in our regiment was knocked down by a cannonball. It struck his gun and broke it all to pieces but did not hurt him very much. We had to drop to the ground often to save our heads from the shell. The battery was taken from them just as we got there.[13]

After a two-mile march, Private Smith and the rest of the men of the 20th Connecticut arrived just north of the Wheat Field, at about 7:00 P.M. Here the men of the 5th and 20th Connecticut relieved the exhausted Nutmeggers of the 27th as Williams replaced General Caldwell's division along the fringes of the Wheat Field. Colonel Wooster quickly ordered his regiment into battle line. Nearby the 5th Connecticut also deployed and prepared to attack, but these Connecticut Yankees never clashed with Longstreet's Confederates; they "were placed in position, but before becoming engaged the enemy were repulsed."[14]

Soon the battle lines along Cemetery Ridge stabilized for the night. Meade quickly reorganized and strengthened his defensive line along the western slopes of the hill and then ordered Williams to hustle his troops back to their original position on Culp's Hill. Meade knew the risks involved in stripping that hill of Williams's divisions, but he had to save the situation in the Wheat Field and along the base of Little Round Top. After this readjustment he could concentrate again on protecting his right flank. By the time Williams reversed his division and retraced his route to Culp's Hill, his men had been tramping back and forth for at least five hours. Lt. John W. Storrs of the 20th Connecticut described the situation awaiting the division as it approached Culp's Hill:

> Winding our way back, amid the darkness, we reached the vicinity of our first position about 10 o'clock P.M.,

and then learned that the enemy were in possession of our rifle pits. General Williams halted near the Baltimore Pike, deployed into line, and sent forward skirmishers, expecting to find but a small force of the enemy. But the heavy musketry fire that greeted our men told plainly that the Rebels were there in force and that only a battle would give us possession of the works again.[15]

The Southerners had worked their way across Rock Creek and into the breastworks left virtually unoccupied while Williams's troops were absent. Gen. George S. Greene commanded the few Twelfth Corps regiments left on Culp's Hill when Williams vacated the works. When Williams's men returned from Cemetery Ridge, they learned that a lively engagement had erupted during their absence and that General Greene had furnished enough martial entertainment to tire out their Rebel adversaries. "After about three hours' continuous fighting," they rested in the breastworks on the eastern side of the hill.[16]

Greene's defense of Culp's Hill was a masterpiece of military leadership. He was ordered by General Slocum to remain and "occupy the breastworks thrown up by the corps,"[17] but he had only his own brigade augmented by three borrowed regiments to perform this task. He had little time to extend his lines through the vacated works, for as he stretched a thin defense toward the eastern perimeter of the hill, a regiment on picket duty was driven in by a vigorous Confederate attack. General Johnson's division finally moved across Rock Creek, and once his skirmishers discovered that the lower tier of breastworks was deserted the entire division charged up the hill in force.

Once the Confederates reached the works, they began to claw their way to the summit, feeling their way through the defenses built by General Williams's First Division. They came dangerously close to the Baltimore Pike, but since it was pitch black by then they stopped short of that important road. The Rebels instead concentrated on reaching the summit of Culp's Hill. As they steadily moved forward, Greene's regiments harried them in the dark, each Northerner firing as often as he could while slowly pulling back to the top of the hill. While his troops were delaying the Rebel advance, Greene improvised a defensive line near the summit extending to the right toward the Baltimore Pike. He manned this line with the few reserves at hand, "which checked any further advance of the enemy on the right."[18] He hoped to contain the Rebels in the works below the summit and prevent them from reaching the Baltimore Pike. He succeeded, and by chance he gained the help of a brigade commanded by Gen. Thomas Kane to ensure that success.

In the late afternoon of 2 July, when Williams set out for Cemetery Ridge with what he believed to be his entire two divisions, Brigadier General Kane, following the unit directly ahead of him, took his men in the wrong direction. His was the last brigade to march down the pike to the rear. Kane soon sensed that his brigade was moving away from the fight, and he countermarched his men back toward Culp's Hill. It was dark by the time he reached the position that had been held by the First Division of the Twelfth Corps. Now Johnson's Confederates controlled that area, and Rebel pickets began to fire on Kane's men. Greene heard the small arms fire, guessed that a friendly unit was involved, and sent an officer to conduct Kane's brigade along the turnpike to a new defensive position near the top of the hill. Kane settled his brigade in next to Greene's regiments. The Confederates, still pressing on to the trenches and groping toward the summit, knew that reinforcements had joined the Federal regiments along the hilltop. Greene noted that the presence of Kane's brigade "tended to render the enemy cautious, and they rested on their arms till morning."[19]

In Greene's immediate front the fighting simmered down for the night. But down the hill near Rock Creek and Spangler's Spring, sporadic rifle fire punctuated the night. When Gen. Thomas A. Ruger led his First Division from Cemetery Ridge back to Culp's Hill, he soon discovered that the breastworks he previously occupied were in Confederate hands.

Ruger halted his men along the Baltimore Pike just south of Spangler's Spring and then decided to prod the southern extremities of the hill with a few skirmishers to determine if it was possible to return to his old position. Looking to the 5th Connecticut to provide the men, within minutes Colonel Packer had 14 volunteers—led by Capt. Alfred A. Chinery of Norwalk—ready to reconnoiter. Packer later wrote that "Their instructions were not to fire upon or otherwise alarm the enemy, but merely to ascertain and report their position. In endeavoring to carry out these instructions, five enlisted men of my command were taken prisoners; others coming in reported our works occupied by the enemy in heavy force."[20]

Another member of the regiment also managed to get captured—Chaplain Moses C. Welch of Hartford, who somehow managed to join the skirmishers. However, for Welch, this initial misfortune had a happy ending. On 7 August 1863 Colonel Packer sent a letter to Connecticut's governor, William A. Buckingham, reviewing the operations of the 5th Connecticut in the Gettysburg campaign. He closed his report praising the conduct and good deeds of "the esteemed chaplain of this regiment, Rev. M. C. Welch." Packer then noted that Welch "was invariably found in the front, whenever the regiment or any portion of it occupied a position of danger or responsibility, encouraging the men by his presence . . . once taken prisoner, but making his escape and reporting immediately for the duties of his position." Packer wrote that Welch escaped, but the regimental record states that the chaplain was "released from captivity on July 4, 1863." Possibly the Rebels respected Welch as a "man of the cloth" or honored him for his daring—perhaps both. Either way, Welch was not in the hands of the Confederates for more than two days. The chaplain continued to serve with the regiment until 5 July 1864, when he resigned his commission.[21]

When Williams combined the information received from his skirmishers with Greene's report of his struggle, he knew that he had to prepare a strong offensive to regain his trenches. This Connecticut-born general wasted no time in placing his infantry and artillery in a semicircular arrangement around the breastworks on the lower southeastern face of Culp's Hill, their backs to the Baltimore Pike.[22] Slocum and Williams knew that if the Confederates broke through to the Baltimore Pike, they would endanger the Federal troops along Cemetery Ridge by taking them in reverse.

When Williams completed the deployment of the Twelfth Corps, the bulk of the First and Second divisions lay between the Rebel line and the Baltimore Pike. The 20th Connecticut first took position on the left of the First Brigade as a reserve in the second line, "but General Ruger, commanding the division, knowing the desperate character of the contest about to take place, specially directed that a regiment that had been placed in the front line should be relieved, and that the 20th should take the post of honor on the left of his front division line, thus showing his appreciation of the regiment." As the rest of Colonel McDougall's brigade worked its way into position on the right of the 20th Connecticut, Colonel Wooster ordered Company G to advance as skirmishers "to a line near the woods, and so it remained during the night, at intervals engaging the enemy's skirmishers."[23] With their skirmishers out front along the fringe of woods hiding the breastworks, the remainder of the 20th Connecticut "lay on its arms in a cornfield" drawn up in battle line and prepared to work toward the trenches when so ordered.

Before daybreak on 3 July, Williams had his Twelfth Corps in position to press the Confederates occupying the breastworks in front of him. He had also placed artillery units where they could rake the Confederates with crossfire before the infantry attacked. The positioning of troops resulted in both the 5th and 20th Connecticut regiments spending the night along the southern crest of the hill. After Colonel Packer drew in his skirmishers, he led the 5th Connecticut to its bivouac area "on the crest of the hill just west of Spangler's Spring." Packer reported that as his regiment moved in that direction "we received a volley from the enemy's skirmishers. No damage was done, however, having reached the crest of the hill, we passed the night in that position."[24]

Gen. Robert E. Lee knew on the morning of 3 July that he had the strength to mount one more attack against the Union forces. His plan called for a solid thrust against the center of

Meade's line on Cemetery Ridge. Before sunrise a courier rode toward Ewell's headquarters with orders that the general complete his mission, engage the Federal forces around Culp's Hill, and strike through their defenses to the Baltimore Pike. Given a third opportunity to overrun the hills in his sector of the battlefield, Ewell's task was to neutralize the Twelfth Corps and come down hard on the Federal units in his area as Lee began his great charge led by Gen. George E. Pickett's fresh division. Before the courier could reach Ewell's headquarters, Lee was startled by a sudden eruption of heavy cannon fire around Culp's Hill.[25] A Connecticut general had rearranged the timetable, and his Yankees were poised to push Ewell's divisions back across Rock Creek. The artillery prelude dropped shot and shell from 26 cannons on the breastworks and woods occupied by Johnson's brigades. Unable to move against such a pounding, the Rebels sought whatever cover the woods and trenches provided and waited for the inevitable infantry assault.

After 15 or 20 minutes Williams halted the bombardment and signaled his infantry to attack. But the Rebels were already on the move, springing forward through the woods, darting toward the Baltimore Pike, and scrambling up the slopes of the hill. Again Williams called for artillery, and again the 26 guns opened fire across the wooded hillsides. The men in the 20th Connecticut were among the Federal troops edging their way under fire toward the Confederate breastworks, and some Northern artillery shells fell short, landing instead on the Nutmeggers. Whether the fault lay in bad fuses or confused range-finding made little difference to Colonel Wooster. The crusty commander "sent word to the batterymen, that, if it was allowed to continue, he would turn the regiment on them. And he was just the man to keep his word."[26]

Although the 5th and 20th Connecticut were brigaded together under Colonel McDougall as units in the First Division, Twelfth Corps, they were assigned dissimilar roles in this day's action. Colonel Packer's 5th Connecticut engaged in a series of defensive maneuvers designed to prevent the

Rebels from reaching the Baltimore Pike. Meanwhile, Colonel Wooster led the 20th Connecticut into a hornet's nest of small-arms fire that blanketed every wooded quarter on the eastern slopes of Culp's Hill.[27]

Williams had positioned the First Division so that its brigades extended from Rock Creek west along the marshes and low-lying reaches of Culp's Hill, with the Baltimore Pike to their rear. General Ruger temporarily commanded this division. He anchored the right of Col. Silas Colgrove's Third Brigade along Rock Creek and spread its regiments in a semicircle around the marshes neighboring the creek. The First Brigade on Colgrove's left flank continued the line into the wooded areas of the hills facing north. The 20th Connecticut held down the left flank of Colonel McDougall's First Brigade, and it was from this position that Colonel Wooster took his Yankees forward to probe the defenses of the Confederates occupying the Union trenches.[28]

No Federal units occupied the area on the immediate left of the 20th Connecticut. During the early hours of the morning, Brig. Gen. Henry B. Lockwood moved his Second Brigade of the First Division to the right of General Greene's makeshift defensive line near the top of the hill. Lockwood's right flank now rested near the Baltimore Pike. A gap of 200 or 300 yards existed between Lockwood's position and the 20th Connecticut farther down the hill. The Confederates of Gen. George Steuart's brigade soon discovered that gap, and once the heavy shelling eased off, they scrambled out of their trenches struggling to force their way around the Yankee left flank and through the gap to the Baltimore Pike. Colonel Wooster reported that "for over five hours parts of my regiment were unceasingly engaged with the enemy, the advanced line frequently relieved from my main line. The enemy were endeavoring to advance through the woods, so as to turn the right flank of the Second Division, and were met and successfully resisted by my regiment."[29]

Often, descriptions of the Battle of Gettysburg pay little attention to the fierce struggle for Culp's Hill waged during the early morning hours of 3 July. This fight is frequently portrayed as no more than a preliminary to the grand encounter later in the day when General Pickett led his Southern legions parade-ground style up the western slopes of Cemetery Ridge. In truth, the conflict for Culp's Hill engaged thousands of soldiers in a bitter contest fought from behind trees and boulders in a maze of underbrush, trenches, and breastworks.

In this struggle the 20th Connecticut played a most incisive role. Johnson knew that Ewell and Lee expected him to drive over Culp's Hill, neutralize the effectiveness of the Federal troops in that area, and break through their defenses to the Baltimore Pike. When morning light began to filter through the leaves overhead, the Confederates were finally able to see what lay around them. The Union barrage moderated at about 5:00 A.M., and the Confederates moved from the trenches, up the slopes, and toward the pike. Johnson sent every brigade available to him against the Union lines. General Steuart's mission was to move his Rebel brigade from the breastworks built by the 20th Connecticut and the other regiments of McDougall's brigade, push through the gap on the left of the 20th Connecticut, and fight his way to the Baltimore Pike. Protecting Steuart's left flank near Rock Creek were several regiments of Walker's brigade positioned to butt up against Colgrove's Union brigade when the Confederates came out of their trenches. In addition to four brigades of his own division, Johnson now commanded three additional brigades from other Confederate divisions. These were led by Brig. Gen. William "Extra Billy" Smith, Col. E. A. O'Neal, and Brig. Gen. Junius Daniel.[30] Each of these three brigades moved into line and supported Johnson's all-out thrust toward the pike.

The mission of McDougall's brigade was to recapture the trenches abandoned the previous evening. General Ruger, commanding McDougall's division, had placed the Connecticut regiment on the left flank of the assaulting team. After the artillery had fired for at least an hour, Colonel Wooster moved his Connecticut regiment up the southern slope of Culp's Hill. At the same time Steuart's Confederates made their advance. A clash was inevitable and immediate, and a series of sporadic advances and retreats began. Later, Colonel McDougall noted that Wooster had an arduous and responsible mission to perform:

> For several hours this regiment occupied a most important position in these woods south of our line of entrenchments in preventing the enemy getting around the right of General Geary's forces in the entrenchments on our left, and holding back the enemy so that our artillery could have free play upon his columns without destroying our own troops.[31]

As the 20th Connecticut moved forward, the other regiments of McDougall's brigade did likewise. Each regiment, intent on regaining its original position behind the breastworks, sought whatever cover the woods afforded. The entire brigade guided on the 20th Connecticut as Wooster's Yankees reached for the brow of the hill. On several occasions Wooster pressed his men forward in advance of his support. His mission included providing information to the artillery as the Federal batteries attempted to pinpoint Confederate positions in the woods. He reported that in his advanced position he was "enabled to repeatedly communicate to the colonel commanding the brigade and the general commanding the division the movements of the enemy in our immediate front, thereby enabling our artillery to more accurately obtain the range of the enemy and to greatly increase the effectiveness of our shells."[32] The horror and shock created by a shell when it tore into a man etched permanent scars on the mind and body of Pvt. George W. Warner of Company B of the 20th Connecticut. This soldier "suffered the terrible loss of both arms by the bursting of a shell, though, strange to say, he was unaware that he had lost but one limb until coming soon after under the hand of Surgeon J. Wadsworth Terry, when he coolly remarked, 'Why Surgeon, I've lost my right arm too! I thought I had only lost my left.' "[33]

Confronted by increasingly heavy Rebel fire, and sometimes hit by their own artillery, the men of the 20th now managed to gain the brow of the hill. Directly below them were the breastworks they had constructed the previous day;

they were still occupied by the Confederates. Gradually, Wooster's Yankees worked their way to a stone wall that ran roughly parallel to the breastworks a few rods farther down the hill. Using the wall as a jumping-off point, they prepared to advance again, and, in Colonel Wooster's words, "now a charge would be made and the line of works reached; then an overwhelming force of rebels advancing would drive our men out and they would take refuge behind the stone wall . . . " Gaining ground in this type of struggle was arduous work. Eventually, Wooster maneuvered his regiment into a position where the Confederates could no longer advance around his left wing, and he then forced a permanent lodging in his own breastworks. On his right flank, the other regiments of Colonel McDougall's brigade soon followed the 20th into their fortified positions. Driven father down the slope by the concentration of fire, Johnson's brigades still mounted charges that took them up to the breastworks, but they could no longer sustain a drive that would clear the Federals from the trenches. The toll in killed and wounded mounted with each Confederate charge. In the words of a soldier in Steuart's brigade, "the men were mowed down with fearful rapidity. . . . It was the most fearful fire I ever encountered. . . . The greatest confusion ensued, regiments were reduced to companies and everything mixed up. It came very near to being a rout . . . "[34]

While McDougall's brigade fought all morning to regain their positions on Culp's Hill, Greene's brigade fought furiously to keep the Confederates from gaining the summit. Greene reported that "the greater part of their heavy losses were sustained within a few yards of our breastworks." He also noted that General Meade had moved a Sixth Corps brigade to his support. Brig. Gen. Alexander Shaler, another native of Connecticut, arrived early in the morning and positioned his regiments behind Greene's brigade to buttress that end of the line. When Shaler reached the summit, Connecticut had two generals fighting to save the hill. General Williams rested easier when Shaler shoved his veterans into line. This Connecticut leader had come up through the ranks, and his general's insignia indicated military ability, not political favoritism. In helping Greene turn back the Confederates, Shaler's brigade did not escape unscathed. Most of his 74 casualties occured on Culp's Hill.[35]

Colonel Wooster and his 20th Connecticut had been under constant pressure for most of the morning. When they regained control of their original breastworks, Colonel McDougall ordered the 123d New York Regiment to relieve the men from Connecticut. Once the New Yorkers occupied the trenches, the exhausted but jubilant Nutmeggers drew back to rest and to replenish their ammunition. As Private Smith noted later: "We marched off about half a mile and commenced cooking coffee." But, as he ruefully continued, "Before some of them had got their fire built we were ordered to fall in an move to some other place so we had to leave without our grub. There is not much time to cook in a battle, I tell you." In spite of Private Smith's frustration, he took comfort in the knowledge that his regiment, and the Twelfth Corps as a whole, had succeeded in clearing the Confederates from the woods and lowlands around Culp's Hill. The right flank of the Federal position was again secure, and Ewell's divisions were in no condition to strike again when Lee needed them in the afternoon. General Greene summed up the situation in a terse statement: "By 10 A.M. the fighting ceased, and at 1 P.M. the enemy had disappeared from our front, and our men went to Rock Creek for water."[36]

The Confederate withdrawal brought a welcome calm in the struggle for control of the hills south of Gettysburg. Occasionally sniper fire alerted the troops that skirmishers were probing enemy positions. But from noontime until 1:30 P.M., the oppressive heat of a burning July sun bathed the sweltering, silent battlefield, and Meade's soldiers rested behind their defensive positions along the entire line from the Round Tops, up across Cemetery Ridge, and over Culp's Hill. The waiting became as oppressive as the noonday heat. Union officers scanned the horizon for signs of Confederate activity while a few regiments and batteries shifted positions to strengthen the line. The 5th Connecticut had moved about all morning to buttress apparent weaknesses in Union positions around Culp's Hill.

Colonel Packer's Connecticut regiment spent the night of 2 July near the crest of Culp's Hill and remained in that position as a reserve regiment until midmorning on 3 July. Then Packer led his regiment "back about half a mile, for the purpose of watching the movements of the enemy upon our right." His orders placed him at the foot of McAllister's Hill in support of Winneger's battery near the Baltimore Pike and adjacent to Rock Creek. He spread his regiment around the northern base of the hill and moved his skirmishers forward and along the bank of the creek. They met no serious opposition, but sporadic fire from Confederate sharpshooters kept them constantly alert. Meanwhile, Winneger's artillerymen atop the hill were unmolested as they raked the Rebels with shot and shell from their 12-pounders.[37] Packer's new position brought his regiment up behind the right regiments of Colonel Colgrove's brigade. Colgrove's right flank reached to the creek, and when the 5th Connecticut backed them up two of Colgrove's regiments began to move across a nearby swale separating them from the Confederate skirmishers of the two brigades led by Generals Walker and Smith. A hot encounter proved very costly to Colgrove's infantry, but after the fight the Rebels began to withdraw. Colgrove's demonstration convinced Johnson that he could not push his way through the Northern regiments protecting the Baltimore Pike.

When the battle for Culp's Hill ended, Williams's command rested for an hour or two, savoring their success against the troops once led by Stonewall Jackson. At 1:30 P.M., the general and his tired divisions caught the sound of cannonading as 140 Confederate artillery pieces opened on Cemetery Ridge. An immediate response from Union artillery exploded from almost as many cannon, heralding the greatest bombardment of the Civil War. As the intensity of the shelling increased, the Union soldiers on Culp's Hill manned their positions along the slopes ready to throw back any possible attack. But none took place.

Throughout the bombardment that afternoon, the Connecticut Yankees remained in the positions last assigned them after the Confederates withdrew. The 5th Connecticut

Fig. 9. Veterans of the 17th Connecticut who fought with Major Brady at the Benner Farm, *from top left:* Pvt. Charles M. Pendleton, Co. A (Courtesy Karl Sundstrom); Lt. Marcus Waterbury, Co. B (Courtesy *MOLLUS*); and Pvt. James C. Hoyt, Co. F (Courtesy *MOLLUS*).

Fig. 10. Adj. Albert H. Wilcoxson, 17th Connecticut.
Courtesy Walter L. Powell.

Fig. 11. Cpl. DeWitt Ruscoe, Co. H, 17th Connecticut.
Courtesy New Canaan Historical Society.

Fig. 12. Pvt. Justus Silliman, Co. H, 17th Connecticut.
Courtesy New Canaan Historical Society.

Fig. 13. Lt. Col. Henry Merwin, 27th Connecticut. Photograph reprinted from Jerome B. Lucke, *History of the New Haven Grays* (1876).

Fig. 14. Veterans of Culp's Hill, *from left:* Lt. Alex H. Buckingham, Co. G, 20th Connecticut; Lt. George N. Raymond, Co. A, 5th Connecticut; Capt. Henry W. Dayboll, Co. G, 5th Connecticut. Courtesy *MOLLUS.*

Fig. 15. Pvt. George W. Warner, Co. B, 20th Connecticut.
Courtesy Tom Riemor.

Fig. 16. Breastworks at Culp's Hill (ca. 15 July 1863).
Courtesy William A. Frassanito.

Fig. 17. Foot of East Cemetery Hill (1882).
Courtesy Gettysburg National Park.

Fig. 18. Maj. Theodore G. Ellis, 14th Connecticut.
Courtesy *MOLLUS.*

Fig. 19. Capt. James Coit, 14th Connecticut. Courtesy *MOLLUS*.

Fig. 20. Bryan Farm and Cemetery Ridge (ca. 1882).
Courtesy Gettysburg National Park.

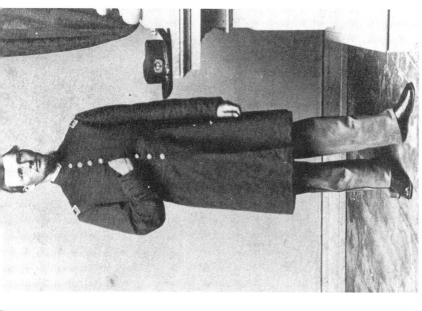

Fig. 21. Sgt. George Lewis, Co. F, 14th Connecticut (Courtesy Walter Powell) and Assistant Surgeon Levi Jewett, 14th Connecticut (Courtesy MOLLUS).

Fig. 22. Capt. Samuel A. Moore. Courtesy *MOLLUS*.

Fig. 23. Veterans of the 14th
Connecticut at Cemetery
Ridge, *from top left:* Lt. James
F. Simpson, Co. D; Sgt. Julius
W. Knowlton, Co. C; Charles
E. Penhallow, Co. D. Courtesy
*MOLLUS.*

Fig. 24. Capt. John C. Broatch, Co. A, 14th Connecticut.
Courtesy Tom Riemor.

rested close to Rock Creek at the foot of McAllister's Hill. The 20th was stationed a little to the rear of its original position in the breastworks. Pulled from the front line, Colonel Wooster's men now held a reserve position adjacent to the Baltimore Pike. Lt. John W. Storrs sketched in his notes a word picture of the activity behind the lines during the bombardment of Cemetery Ridge:

> When the rebel fire opened, the whole "debris," the loose material of the army, which during the forenoon had gathered up towards the left to get out of range while the battle raged on the right, could be seen rushing to the rear with accelerated speed. Officers, servants, orderlies, clerks, musicians, ambulance drivers, etc. came down the hill at double quick. It seemed as if half the army was running away, but it was only the non-combatants; amid the storm of missiles, the union line remained firm and unbroken.[38]

Later on in the afternoon, General Meade moved his headquarters to Power's Hill across the Baltimore Pike from Culp's Hill. Here he shared General Slocum's headquarters beyond the range of most of Lee's guns. The tremendous barrage of Confederate explosives generally overshot Cemetery Ridge, creating havoc among the supply units and reserve contingents on the reverse side of the hill. The men of the 20th were also caught in this fire—something Pvt. Abner Smith recalled vividly: "They played at us the best they knew how for about three hours. We were in the woods at the time and no one knew but each minute was his last. The shells flew thick and fast. They struck all around me, burst and fly in all directions."[39]

When the bombardment subsided and the Union counter-battery fire ceased, Meade knew what to expect next and hastened to support his infantry along Cemetery Ridge, for General Pickett awaited Longstreet's command and was poised to lead some 12,000 men in a gallant charge towards Cemetery Ridge. Feeling that Culp's Hill was now secure, Meade again ordered units of the Twelfth Corps to march to

Cemetery Ridge. As the Northern artillery opened a merciless fire on the advancing Confederates, the 20th Connecticut fell into marching position with the rest of the brigade. Again the unit retraced some of its steps of the previous evening. Lieutenant Storrs wrote,

> Moving up the Baltimore Pike, through a perfect storm of shell fire from the batteries of the enemy as a cover for his retreating and decimated forces, a staff officer was met just before the brigade arrived at the designated point, who conveyed an order from General Meade for it to return to its former position, as the enemy had been repulsed at all points and was flying from the field.[40]

Reversing its direction, the Connecticut regiment plodded back to Culp's Hill, exhausted by 24 hours of fighting, marching, and countermarching. But these were now jubilant men, joining in the cheering that rolled along the entire line. Again Meade's army had absorbed Lee's heavy assault and turned his legions away for the last time at Gettysburg. Colonel Wooster's Yankees settled into their breastworks along Culp's Hill, content in the thought that their efforts helped General Meade gain his great victory.

Meanwhile the 5th Connecticut maintained its position near McAllister's Hill, detached from the movements of McDougall's brigade. At about 6:00 P.M. General Slocum took precautionary measures to protect the right flank of the Northern army. Soon Colonel Packer's regiment received orders "to report with the Thirteenth New Jersey as support for General Gregg's cavalry who were protecting the extreme right of our army. We moved off about 2 miles and stopped for the night."[41] Theirs was a reconnaissance mission to determine whether or not General Johnson had abandoned the field. Moving along the Bonaughtown Road, the 5th Connecticut and the 13th New Jersey met no resistance. Soon the detachment reached Gregg's picket line and bedded down with the cavalry for the night.

# 6

## "The Last Throw of the Dice"

## The 14th Connecticut & the Fight for Cemetery Ridge

You could mark the path that they took by the dead
   that they left behind,
Spilled from that deadly march, as a cart spills meal
   on a road.
      —Stephen Vincent Benét, *John Brown's Body*

AFTER THE BATTLE OF GETTYSBURG, Gen. Robert E. Lee might
have written the following lines:

> There are impossibilities in warfare—things that no
> troops can accomplish, however brave they may be.
> They cannot for one thing cross long stretches of open
> country without any cover in the face of an artillery fire
> of any magnitude, and then clamber up a hill-side ex-
> posed to the musketry of concealed foe, and then cross
> the ditches and scale the earthworks of the enemy, driv-
> ing the latter from their position with the bayonet. . . .
> The latter, lying under cover, firing from a place of safety
> may murder your men. You may try again and again the
> experiment, but each repetition only lengthens the
> butcher's bill.[1]

But these were not Lee's sentences. They were penned by
William T. Lusk and sent to his mother in Norwich on
16 December 1862, six months before Gettysburg. Lusk
learned this lesson at Fredericksburg. General Lee did not,
and his battle plan for the third day at Gettysburg called for

his infantry to cross nearly a mile of open terrain and smash into the Union center after 140 of his cannon had bombarded the area. In concert with this attack, General Ewell had been ordered to strike the Union Twelfth Corps at Culp's Hill. Longstreet did not like Lee's plan, and said so. Once again he argued for a flanking movement to the south and east of the Round Tops. And for the second time in 24 hours Lee told his trusty old comrade-in-arms to prepare his divisions for a head-on assault against Cemetery Ridge.[2]

Late in the evening of 2 July, after the fighting had diminished, General Meade called in his commanders for a council of war. They met in the widow Lydia Leister's tiny farmhouse that Meade had been using for his headquarters, and after each of his generals advised a continued defense of their present positions, Meade decided to strengthen his lines and await another attack. As Brig. Gen. John Gibbon, temporary commander of the Second Corps, left the farmhouse, Meade told him that he expected Lee to attack the center of the Union line the following day. This was Gibbon's sector, and it ranged along Cemetery Ridge from Ziegler's Grove on the north to a little south of the now-well-known "clump of trees." Meade explained to Gibbon that Lee had already attempted to smash in both Federal flanks and failed. Next, he would try to cut through the middle of the Union line, separate its flanks, and, in turn, overwhelm them.[3] Meade had read Lee correctly. Early in the morning of 3 July, General Gibbon rode along the line of his command and warned division leaders about the probability of a general assault against their front. Already the guns were roaring to their rear in the area of Culp's Hill, where a diversionary attack might well be under way.

On the previous morning, Brig. Gen. Alexander Hays had spurred his horse up and down the ridge shouting orders to his brigade commanders as he positioned the Third Division of the Second Corps. A flamboyant but extremely capable military leader, Hays pushed his regiments into the sector assigned to them by the army's left wing commander, General Hancock. Facing his troops toward the west, Hays stretched his ranks from Ziegler's Grove south along a stone wall to a point just short of where the wall took a 90-degree turn west. There, in a field about 200 yards behind the wall, the Yankees of the 14th Connecticut had halted. Their regiment brought up the rear of Col. Thomas A. Smyth's Second Brigade, and strung out ahead of it were the 1st Delaware, 12th New Jersey, and 108th New York. Smyth placed the New York regiment, heading the column, in support of Woodruff's brass cannon, facing west on the fringe of Ziegler's Grove. Detachments from the remaining regiments were moved to establish a skirmish line across the Emmitsburg Road. Most of Connecticut's infantrymen remained in the field directly behind the Bryan farmhouse until late in the afternoon, "the men keeping their accouterments on and remaining close by their stacks of arms."[4]

Here in this field the 14th Connecticut suffered its first casualty at Gettysburg. Capt. James Coit of Norwich was struck down by the hooves of a runaway horse, not by Confederate fire. A drummer boy, instructed to take the horse to the rear, lost control of the animal when it panicked during artillery fire. The horse plunged down the field, cut a swath through scattering soldiers, and bore down on Coit. He tried to fend off the horse with his sword, but the full weight of the animal struck him in the face and chest, driving him to the ground. Bruised and injured, Coit was helped to a field hospital.[5] In a few days he was able to return to duty, but whatever he knew of the great Confederate charge on 3 July he learned from his comrades.

Late in the afternoon of 2 July, the Connecticut 14th moved about two hundred yards further toward the left, passing through an apple orchard and halting on its further edge, quite near the headquarters of General Hays, commanding the division. Here the regiment was placed behind a loosely constructed stone wall. . . . This was the ground occupied by the regiment during the rest of the battle. This arrangement made it face the west and occupy the ground which had been filled by the New York brigade.[6]

On that same afternoon, General Longstreet had reluctantly committed his brigades in an assault from Devil's Den through the Wheat Field to the Peach Orchard. The attack reached its climax along the Emmitsburg Road, where Northern general Andrew Humphreys led his division in a valiant attempt to thwart a Confederate effort to crack his lines and reach Cemetery Ridge. General Hancock quickly sensed the danger of Humphreys's position and ordered Col. George Willard's New York brigade to vacate its position behind the wall and rush to Humphreys's support. As Willard moved out, the 14th Connecticut and other regiments of the Second Brigade moved in behind the wall. The New Yorkers were soon engaged, but the vicious fighting sapped their strength and took the life of Colonel Willard. When his shattered regiments returned to their original sector, General Hays placed the brigade in reserve about 200 feet behind the 14th Connecticut's position along the wall.[7]

After the Battle of Fredericksburg, Maj. Theodore G. Ellis had assumed command of these Connecticut Yankees. Seasoned by fighting at Fredericksburg and Chancellorsville, Ellis proved to be a capable regimental leader at Gettysburg. A native of Hartford and a successful civil engineer, he had been selected as adjutant when the regiment first mustered for federal service. In early campaigning with the unit, Ellis had earned the respect of his fellow soldiers. "Cool, intrepid, unshrinking in the severest contest, he caused the men he led to repose entire confidence in his management." Though usually genial, he became at times caustic in situations where a soldier's reaction or a regimental response was not to his liking.[8]

On 2 July when Ellis moved his regiment up along the wall overlooking the Emmitsburg Road, he quickly ordered skirmishers down the slope of Cemetery Ridge and across the road separating the Union and Confederate positions, assigning Companies A and F to this duty. Toward nightfall four privates from Company A moved aggressively toward a barn on the William Bliss property, about midway between the established positions of both armies, when suddenly a group of

Confederates rose from the tall grain, surrounded Henry Cooley, William Jacobs, James French, and John Geatly, and captured them. These were the first casualties suffered by the regiment near the Bliss Farm, which would figure so prominently in the regiment's activities on 3 July. For the moment, the rest of the 14th Connecticut, sheltered behind their section of wall on Cemetery Ridge, escaped loss, and as dusk shrouded the fields, the men of the regiment sought rest. Elnathan B. Tyler of Middletown, a member of Company B remembered, "That night as we lay, our knapsacks plumb up to the base of the stone wall and pillowed our heads thereon, not being allowed to divest ourselves of any other arms or equipment, we sought for the rest and sleep we so much needed. Arnold's Rhode Island Battery just to the left of us finally quieted down, although I think we could have slept notwithstanding that."[9]

Sergeant Tyler also noted that early in the morning of 3 July his company along with Company D moved out to the skirmish line, relieving Companies A and F. The reserve line for the skirmishers was "the little depression of the Emmitsburg road," and from this position "those of us detailed to go out on the line crawled out across the wheat field to the fence beyond and lying upon the ground behind the posts and lower rails of the fence, began the sharp-shooters drill of the day." This "drill" could quickly turn into a deadly affair as the opposing picket lines, hidden from view by standing grain, played a cat-and-mouse game. A rising sun soon turned the entire field into a sweltering arena where an occasional puff of smoke marked the position of a picket. Such a tell-tale sign brought return fire, and one such outburst took the life of Cpl. Samuel Huxham of Company B, a native of Middletown, who was shot through the head as he rose to a kneeling position to get off a shot at a Confederate.[10] Along each regimental front in the open fields to the west of Cemetery Ridge similar encounters continued throughout the morning.

Meanwhile, Union officers riveted their eyes on Confederate activity up and down Seminary Ridge. There the Southerners were massing artillery, and a growing line of guns stretched northward from the Peach Orchard to a point opposite Ziegler's Grove, just to the right of the 14th Connecticut. Lee was setting the stage for a heavy bombardment of the Union line. Then, after artillery fire had devastated the Federal position and demoralized the troops, accepted military tactics called for Rebel infantry to storm whatever remained of Union opposition. Generations of fighting men fought and died under these antique rules, even when progress in weaponry turned such a technique into wholesale butchery. Longstreet hated the thought of sacrificing his divisions in another "old style" assault, but Lee was adamant. If his battle plans were properly executed by all elements of his command, his infantry would prove invincible. Consequently, while the Confederate cannons were wheeling into line, Longstreet ordered those infantry divisions chosen to form in line. By noon, more than 12,000 Confederate infantry were in position. Every Southern soldier knew that success depended on the smashing of Federal cannons prior to the infantry advance, and with it the demoralization of Meade's infantry by the bombardment. Lee was confident of a Confederate victory; Longstreet was not.[11]

Confederate and Federal soldiers told of a quiet morning along the opposing ridges on 3 July—that is, relatively quiet after the heavy fighting of the day before. But up and down the skirmish line in the fields between Cemetery and Seminary ridges, pickets and sharpshooters broke the silence from time to time as they continued to play their deadly game. At 10:00 A.M. the action heated up directly in front of the wall protecting the 14th Connecticut. Within minutes the entire regiment became involved in a nasty fight in the land between the ridges.[12]

About 400 yards beyond the Emmitsburg Road lay the Bliss barn and farmhouse, bordered by a 10-acre orchard and a field of wheat. Here William Bliss, a native of Massachusetts, had moved in 1857; he owned nearly 60 acres of land. Like other farms in the area, the most imposing structure on his property was a substantial barn—75 feet long and 35 feet wide. It had a solid-oak frame encased by stone on the first floor and brick on the second floor, and it had several doors, windows,

Fig. 25. Lt. Frederick S. Seymour, Co. I, 14th Connecticut.
Courtesy Tom Riemor.

Fig. 26. Sgt. Maj. William B. Hincks. Courtesy Tom Riemor.

Fig. 27. Capt. Samuel Fiske, Co. G, 14th Connecticut.
Courtesy Tom Riemor.

Fig. 28. Lt. Wilbur D. Fisk, Co. F, 14th Connecticut.
Courtesy Tom Riemor.

Fig. 29. Lt. James R. Nichols, Co. K, 14th Connecticut.
Courtesy Tom Riemor.

Fig. 30. Sgt. Franklin Bartlett, Co. A, 14th Connecticut.
Courtesy Tom Riemor.

Fig. 31. Dedication of the 17th Connecticut monument, 1 July 1884. Courtesy Lewis Leigh.

Fig. 32. 14th Connecticut veterans at East Cemetery Hill, 15 September 1891. Photograph reprinted from Henry S. Stevens, *Souvenir of the Excursion to Battlefields . . .* (1893).

and vents. Because of its sound masonry construction, the barn became a miniature fortress, and here Union and Confederate skirmishers struggled for its possession throughout the previous day. By midmorning on 3 July, Confederate sharpshooters again had control and were picking off some of the men of Capt. Arnold's Rhode Island battery. Several times on 2 July detachments of the 12th New Jersey and 1st Delaware regiments of Smyth's brigade were ordered to advance to the barn and secure it, and twice their missions were successful. In the afternoon the 12th New Jersey captured the barn and took 92 prisoners, but they left the barn intact, and as soon as the men withdrew, the Confederates occupied the buildings again.[13]

When the sun's rays silhouetted Federal officers and artillerymen along Cemetery Ridge on the morning of 3 July, Confederate sharpshooters resumed their activity, causing enough trouble to draw the attention of Gen. Alexander Hays. Despite another assault by the 12th New Jersey, the Confederates had returned, and this time Hays ordered Colonel Smyth to rid his troops permanently of this vexation. Smyth called upon the 14th Connecticut, and as the regiment prepared to move out, Captain Arnold suggested to Smyth that both buildings be burned. Mindful of General Hays's order to secure the buildings and "to stay," Smyth was hesitant. But as he escorted Company C of the regiment as far as the Emmitsburg Road, Lt. Frederick S. Seymour of Waterbury made the same suggestion, and this time Smyth relented. As Seymour moved to the head of his company to lead the advance, Smyth rode over to him and said, "If they make it too hot for you, burn the buildings and return to the line." Unfortunately, no one else heard Smyth's order, and as Seymour moved forward he was badly wounded and did not convey the message.[14]

Behind the wall on Cemetery Ridge the rest of the 14th Connecticut watched pensively as Capt. Samuel A. Moore moved four companies toward the Bliss buildings. Sixty Nutmeggers followed him as he led them first behind the wall about 200 yards north to the Bryan house then down a lane that ran down the slope to the Emmitsburg Road. At the road, a good 300 yards separated the column from the buildings.

Captain Moore then passed the word that at his command the soldiers were to break ranks and run for the barn as fast as they could. When Moore sprang forward the entire command raced toward the barn. While heat slowed some of them and rifle fire dropped several more, most of Moore's men reached the outside wall of the barn, where it was impossible for the Confederates to get a bead on them from the inside. In fact "such was the dash and wild fury of the approach that the Confederates left the barn in haste, giving only parting shots. Captain Moore was the first to enter the barn, and the Federal soldiers were soon in full command."[15]

Moore and his exhausted men spread throughout the two-story barn, dropping to the floors and crawling to windows and doors, peering cautiously for the whereabouts of the re-treating Confederates. The Bliss house, 60 yards northeast, sheltered some of the Confederates who had fled the barn. Others were already in the orchard. And just 600 yards to the west lay the full strength of the Confederate line on Seminary Ridge. Captain Moore recognized why his predecessors, the men of the 1st Delaware and 12th New Jersey, had remained in the barn just long enough to take prisoners—the barn was a potential trap. If Moore had any further doubts about leaving, he was quickly reminded of the difficulty of his position when Southern artillery roared into action, bouncing shot and shell off the barn. Hemmed in and outnumbered, the Yankees in the barn could not muster the strength to rush the house, and they were constantly harassed by sharpshooters from the picket line and the Bliss orchard.

Back at Cemetery Ridge, Major Ellis watched with alarm as the Southerners continued their heavy fire on the barn. He knew that his comrades were under orders to stay, but he was convinced that they could not long stand such punishment without additional help. General Hays, also aware of the sit-uation, soon ordered Ellis to reinforce his command and cap-ture the Bliss house with the rest of the regiment. With an effective strength now numbering only 60 men (his last two companies were on the picket line), Ellis directed the color guard to remain at the wall and then alerted his remaining

four companies to follow him down the lane to the Emmitsburg Road. Like Moore, Major Ellis led his detail in a "go as
you please" rush. As soon as Ellis ordered the charge, the
Confederates in the house, the orchard, and along the picket
line opened a savage fire that cut down several of the Nutmeggers. But there was no turning back, even when they
came within range of an unexpected flanking fire poured into
them by volleys from their right. There, in a narrow stretch of
sunken country lane, Gen. E. L. Thomas had positioned his
brigade the previous evening. Several of Ellis's men were hit
by this enfilading fire, "but the majority, heated and panting,
reached the goal, some entering the house and others continuing to the barn."[16]

This courageous advance cleared the immediate area of
Confederate infantrymen, but Ellis quickly recognized that
the house was too frail to withstand both musketry and artillery fire, and most of his remaining men withdrew to the
barn. This point became all too clear when Maj. William Pe-
gram, commanding a battalion of Confederate artillery, ordered Purcell's battery to keep the house and barn under
steady fire once the remaining Southerners had withdrawn
from the area. One of the Rebel cannoneers reported that "the
men were directed to place ten shells beside each of the four
guns of the battery and to continue firing them leisurely at
the buildings until they were vacated. And we fired every one
of those forty shells . . . "[17]

Major Ellis recognized that if he was to remain in the barn
his situation would get increasingly desperate, for even this
sturdy building was not completely secure. At one point a
case shot entered the upper part of the barn and exploded,
killing and wounding several men, including a commissary
sergeant, Julius W. Knowlton of Bridgeport. Ellis was unaware
of the option Colonel Smyth had authorized, to burn the
buildings and withdraw. General Hays, however, remedied Ellis's problem by calling for a volunteer courier to convey the
order. Capt. James Postles of Colonel Smyth's staff came forward and rode toward the Bliss barn. In spite of heavy fire, he
reached the building, shouted the order to Major Ellis, then

spurred his horse again to make a mad dash back for Cemetery Ridge, which he reached safely, saluted by cheers from
friend and foe.[18]

Ellis organized the withdrawal while his men spread hay
and straw about the barn. In the house, straw from mattresses
fueled flames that soon sent smoke curling through windows
and doors. Once the killed and wounded were evacuated, Ellis
led his entire command back to the Emmitsburg Road, where
they halted momentarily to observe the flames consuming
both buildings. No further casualties were suffered in this retreat, but when Major Ellis returned his tired command to its
former position supporting Arnold's battery, there were a lot
fewer men left to defend this section of the stone wall; one-
third of his 160 men were missing.[19]

Indirectly, the Connecticut attack against the Bliss farm
may have contributed to the great Union victory later in the
afternoon on 3 July. In both armies overall control of artillery
fire was slight indeed, but General Hunt did manage to restrain the fire of some Northern batteries during the barrage
preceding "Pickett's Charge." While Hunt had some control,
Lee's artillery chief, Gen. W. N. Pendleton, had none at all.
Consequently, when the 14th Connecticut captured the Bliss
buildings, Purcell's battery was not alone in firing at the
structures. Within minutes all 63 guns of A. P. Hill's Third
Corps opened fire, causing Col. E. P. Alexander, Longstreet's
artillery chief, considerable dismay. He immediately "forbade
his seventy-five guns to have any part in this exchange, because he knew he would need every round of his short supply
of ammunition if he was to clear the way for Pickett and
Pettigrew." Alexander also noted that the barrage against the
Bliss property lasted a good half-hour.[20]

As a scorching sun parched the land between the fated
ridges, and the men upon it, soldiers along both battle lines
took from their knapsacks their meager rations. For thousands of them this was their last meal. Drenched in sweat,
the 14th Connecticut veterans rested and ate in the ominous
silence that hung over that vast field. At 1:00 P.M., two Confederate signal guns broke the stillness, and within seconds
Lee's long line of cannons roared into action, the screaming

shells sending Meade's soldiers diving for whatever cover they could find. The 14th Connecticut veterans crowded up against the wall, pushed together with the men of the 1st Delaware. As the first flights of shells arched toward Cemetery Ridge, Union cannoneers sprang to their guns and pulled the lanyards that sent retaliatory shots ranging towards the Confederates. The greatest artillery barrage of the war had begun.

As the intensity of the shelling increased, Lt. Frank Haskell, aide to General Gibbon, noted that

> Our infantry was still unshaken, and in all the cannonade suffered very little. . . . The batteries had been handled much more severely. . . . A great number of horses had been killed, in some batteries more than half of all. Guns had been dismounted. A great many caissons, limbers and carriages had been destroyed, and usually from ten to twenty-five men to each battery had been struck, at least along our crest. . . . The scenes that meet our eyes on all hands among the batteries were fearful.

Along the front line there was no retreat. Huddled behind their wall, the men of the 14th Connecticut kept close to the ground. Sgt. Maj. William B. Hincks of Bridgeport wrote, "the enemy's guns were pointed so that the shot mainly cleared us and went over the crest of the hill into the valley beyond, where, as we afterwards learned, they supposed our troops were massed," thus sparing most of the wall protecting the 14th Connecticut. Another element favoring the regiment was the terrain immediately below the wall. Built on top of a ledge, the wall could not be undermined by incoming shells. Hincks recorded that shots falling short bounded off the ledge "instead of burying themselves in the ground beneath us and then exploding, tearing in pieces those lying above, as I knew them to do in the grove farther to our right."[21]

The 14th Connecticut escaped the bombardment relatively unscathed, but the men of Arnold's Rhode Island battery were not so lucky. Standing by their guns and working them furiously for more than an hour, the men paid dearly.

Occasionally an incoming shell strayed through the thick smoke and blew up a limber chest or damaged one of the pieces. Lying next to the battery, Sergeant Hincks wrote of the strain of sweating out a heavy bombardment: "One of the guns was directly behind me and at every discharge, the concussion would throw gravel over me and I could not only see and smell the thick cloud of burning powder, but could taste it also. I lay with my arm thrown over Eddy Hart [Sgt. Edward W. Hart of Madison] and so hot was it that the drops of perspiration falling from my face made mud of the dusty soil on which we were stretched. No one moved or spoke save the gunners behind us."[22]

The thundering of Arnold's battery was matched up and down the Federal line by more than 100 other Union guns, including Capt. John W. Sterling's 2d Connecticut Light Battery. Late in the afternoon of the previous day, Captain Sterling had wheeled into line the six guns of his battery, one of several called up from the Artillery Reserve to replace infantry divisions stripped from Cemetery Ridge by General Meade. Brig. Gen. Robert Tyler, commanding the Artillery Reserve, worked feverishly to string out along the lower reaches of the ridge a line of guns to support Federal troops then fighting in the Wheat Field and along the Emmitsburg Road. He personally led Sterling's battery to its position, which would be located in about the center of a line of guns commanded by Col. Freeman McGilvery.[23] Up until now the battery had seen little action. In January 1863 Sterling had moved his battery to Wolf Run Shoals, where it had remained until June as part of the defenses of Washington. On 25 June the Connecticut battery was assigned to the Artillery Reserve of the Army of the Potomac, and once in position at Gettysburg on 2 July it became engaged in its first pitched battle with the enemy—a foretaste of what proved to be its heaviest artillery duel of the war.

On the morning of 3 July, several Union brigades were moved into line as supporting troops for McGilvery's artillery. Most of these men had spent the previous afternoon at the Wheat Field and Peach Orchard, where their losses had been severe. A regiment belonging to Col. Patrick Kelly's

Irish brigade, bloodied in the Wheat Field, settled in next to Sterling's guns. A proud lot of good fighters, the 116th Pennsylvania was now "supporting Sterling's Second Connecticut Battery, the men lying in front of and between the pieces."[24] Up and down the line, soldiers had improved their positions with whatever materials were at hand—fence rails, stones, mounds of earth, shallow trenches. McGilvery's gunners were ready, and so was his supporting infantry.

Captain Sterling's cannoneers had checked their guns and piled their ammunition nearby. When Longstreet's signal guns shattered the noon-hour quiet, Sterling's Yankees scrambled to their cannons, and in less than a minute they were caught up in the great bombardment. Counter–battery fire raised palls of smoke that fogged the field and blinded gunners, and the constant, deafening roar was so overpowering that the artillerymen could not hear the blasts from their own pieces. As the bombardment intensified, Sterling's men noticed that very few enemy shells were exploding in their vicinity, for the Confederates were concentrating their fire further to the north, hoping to silence the cannons defending the walls near the "clump of trees." Occasionally a few shells passed over their heads; one hit a limber chest and blew it to bits, but this was the only piece of equipment that Sterling's men lost during the entire battle.[25]

As the pounding and the thunder of the guns continued, General Hunt became alarmed about the rapid and sometimes indiscriminate shelling by his artillerymen. He knew that enough ammunition had to be conserved to check the Confederate infantry attack that he felt sure would follow the barrage. Reckless of his own safety, Hunt spurred his horse up and down Cemetery Ridge and shouted personal orders to his battery commanders to cease fire. Slowly the rate of fire from Northern guns decreased, then stopped altogether.[26]

About the time that Hunt ordered a cease-fire, Longstreet's artillery chief, Edward Porter Alexander, also began to worry about his ammunition supply. Knowing that his guns would be needed to support the general infantry assault to follow, Alexander sent a staff officer to the ammunition reserves with orders to bring forward what was available. He soon learned that none was within reach; Gen. W. N. Pendleton had removed the ammunition train and reserve batteries to a safer area far to the rear. Moreover, Longstreet had placed upon Alexander's shoulders a most difficult decision, to advise General Pickett to advance when he felt that Union artillery had been sufficiently silenced.[27]

When, under General Hunt's direction, the Federal cannons stopped firing, the Confederate battery commanders assumed they had succeeded, and their guns also fell silent. As the smoke dissipated, Alexander raised his binoculars to discern the condition of the Union positions on Cemetery Ridge. He could make out the wreckage of artillery pieces and limber chests, and he could also see artillerymen and drivers withdrawing guns. He quickly assumed that little if any artillery resistance remained along the front defended by Hancock's Second Corps, the area around the "clump of trees." Alexander was right in assuming that Hancock's batteries had taken a heavy pounding, but the activity he observed was not that of men preparing to withdraw, but of soldiers making preparations to replace damaged pieces with additional cannons and fresh ammunition. Indeed, many batteries had exhausted their supplies of long-range ammunition; Captain Arnold's battery, closest to the 14th, had nothing but canister rounds left—murderous at short range but useless beyond 400 yards. Arnold then withdrew his battery from the line, leaving a void along the wall just to the left of Ellis's regiment. Although artillery from Tyler's reserve had been ordered forward to replace Arnold's battery, they were late in reaching the area. Consequently, Ellis reported that he "moved the regiment forward and to the left, to cover the space previously occupied by the battery."[28] This movement brought the left flank of the Connecticut regiment to within 50 feet of the "inner angle," that point where the wall took a 90-degree turn west, continuing for about 80 yards. Another turn, the "outer angle," carried the wall southward again. In order "to occupy the space at the wall left vacant by the disrupted battery, it was necessary for the regiment to stretch out, leaving only one line."

Once Ellis extended the 14th Connecticut toward the left along the wall, he brought his regiment into contact with the 71st Pennsylvania, the regiment on the right of General Webb's brigade of the Second Division. Two companies of that regiment moved forward after the bombardment to the "outer angle," their right close up in the corner. Once in position, the veterans of the 14th readied themselves for the charge now forming at their front. Confederate regiments shifted to Gen. James Longstreet's temporary command, spearheaded by the Virginia division of Gen. George Edward Pickett, moved into view just about a mile away. All along the rim of Seminary Ridge, brigade after brigade came on line, dressed their positions as if forming for a corps review, and then stepped forward into the blazing sunlight, confident that the impact of their elan and their numbers would give "Marse Robert" the great victory he sought.

The right front of Longstreet's assault column contained three brigades of Pickett's division, and to their rear and in reserve were the brigades of Generals Cadmus M. Wilcox and E. A. Perry. To the left of Pickett, Brig. Gen. Johnston Pettigrew, now in command of Heth's division, raised his arm and waved it toward the "clump of trees" on Cemetery Ridge. Four brigades stepped out into the sunlight, and coming on line each brigade guided right on Col. B. D. Fry's brigade. Behind and in support of Pettigrew, two of Gen. William Dorsey Pender's brigades next marched forward, commanded for the day by Maj. Gen. Isaac Trimble.[29]

Longstreet's striking force, now fully revealed, numbered nine brigades; six were from A. P. Hill's Third Corps, and three were Longstreet's own. In reserve and not then moving forward were two more Third Corps brigades. Directly in front of Col. B. D. Fry's North Carolina brigade lay the "little clump of trees" on Cemetery Ridge, and Fry ordered his Confederates to aim for that point. All other front-line brigades were to dress on Fry. The maneuvering of these troops, perhaps 12,000 in all, was a fascinating pageant of precision, and as they moved forward comments of surprise and admiration came from the lips of Meade's soldiers as they fixed their eyes on this last display of an old-style Napoleonic charge. Major Ellis was moved to write in his official report:

> As far as eye could reach could be seen the advancing troops, their gay war flags fluttering in the gentle summer breeze, while their sabers and bayonets flashed and glistened in the midday sun. Step by step they came, the music and rhythm of their tread resounding upon rock-ribbed earth. Every movement expressed determination and resolute defiance, the line moving forward like a victorious giant, confident of power and victory.... There is no swaying of the line, no faltering of the step. The advance seems as resistless as the incoming tide. It was the last throw of the dice in this supreme moment of the great game of war.[30]

Early adjustments in the line brought Brig. Gen. Garnett's brigade shoulder to shoulder with Fry's brigade. The right of the assault swept down an incline toward the Emmitsburg Road, driving straight toward Colonel McGilvery's cannon. When the Confederates were within range of most of his guns, he snapped his troops from their momentary spell of admiration by screaming, "Fire at will!" The roar of 41 guns wreaked destruction in the ranks of the attacking Confederates. Captain Sterling's men performed so well that Col. St. Clair Mulholland, commander of the 116th Pennsylvania, later recalled that "It was marvelous the rapidity and accuracy with which these guns were served."[31]

As Longstreet's assault got underway, Gen. James L. Kemper's brigade marched on the right of Pickett's division. Virginians all, these were the men moving straight into the mouths of McGilvery's guns. Under severe punishment, the lines of these Confederates suddenly wheeled to the left as Pickett sought to close in on Pettigrew's division and present a unified front in the drive towards Hancock's position on Cemetery Ridge. When Kemper, obeying orders, obliqued his Virginians to the left, he exposed his lines to enfilade fire. The slaughter that followed was best described by Maj. Charles S. Payton of Garnett's brigade, who reported that the Union batteries then "enfiladed nearly an entire line with fearful effect sometimes as many as 10 men being killed or wounded by the bursting of a single shell."[32] This withering artillery fire forced the Confederate infantry to give way to the left, and as they advanced Pickett's brigades began to crowd in on Pettigrew's units heading directly toward the wall shielding the 14th Connecticut and other Second Corps regiments. It was obvious that the Confederates would converge at a point directly in front of Webb's brigade, just to the left of the 14th Connecticut. In front of and to the immediate right of the Connecticut regiment, three of Pettigrew's brigades were driving toward the wall protecting Smyth's brigade.

The blasting of Pickett's right flank by McGilvery's long line of guns forced Kemper's brigade to crowd in on Garnett's regiments after the division had crossed the Emmitsburg Road. This road ran diagonally through the valley west of Cemetery Ridge, close up to the Federal positions in Hancock's sector, but almost twice as far away at the Codori farm buildings where Pickett made his crossing. His brigades were well over the road before Pettigrew on his left reached the fences bordering the narrow dirt roadbed directly in front of the positions manned by Hays's veterans. Quick-witted commanders along the Union line saw the possibility of a double envelopment of the onrushing Confederates, and Brig. Gen. George Stannard sent the 13th and 16th Vermont regiments on the double-quick down the slope in his immediate front. There they got on Kemper's right flank and poured a murderous enfilading fire into his ranks, driving what remained of the brigade still farther to the left, and wounding General Kemper at the same time.[33]

While Stannard was boxing in the right flank of the advancing Confederates, Gen. Alexander Hays rushed additional troops to the opposite flank and extended his line so that his regiments connected with the 8th Ohio on the farther side of the Emmitsburg Road. Just a short time earlier the men of the 8th Ohio, under the command of Col. Franklin Sawyer, had succeeded in flanking and then routing Col. J. M. Brockenbrough's entire brigade as it sought to move forward on the extreme left of the assault. Stannard and Hays had fashioned a slaughter pen into which the Confederates marched. And along the wall just beyond the inner angle, each Connecticut infantryman adjusted the sights of his musket and selected a new target as Pettigrew's riddled brigades neared the fences along the road. They had already driven in the two companies of Connecticut pickets, but, even in the face of this determined advance, the Yankees refused to abandon their wounded comrades. Retreating, but not in confusion, they would "sometimes about face to return the Confederate fire, and thus gain time to bring in the killed and wounded."[34]

To the left of the 14th Connecticut, Lt. Alonzo H. Cushing had run his remaining guns forward to the wall and ordered all canister placed alongside each cannon. When Garnett's brigade came within 400 yards of the wall, Cushing began pumping canister into the Confederates with terrible effect. There is some evidence that one or two of Arnold's guns were also active, for one or two of them were not withdrawn—for lack of horses—when the Confederate bombardment ceased. At most, however, not more than eight or nine artillery pieces supported with canister the infantry regiments of Generals Webb and Hays.[35]

While Northern canister was inflicting severe casualties on the assaulting troops, General Hays ordered his regimental commanders to withhold all musket fire until the Confederates had reached the Emmitsburg Road. There the Southerners would be delayed by the fences bordering the road and would provide excellent targets for Union marksmen at a range of no more than 200–250 yards. Directly in front of the 14th Connecticut and still coming on strong were the regiments of Gen. James Archer's brigade, now led by Colonel Fry. When these Confederates reached the Emmitsburg Road and began to scale the fences, General Hays raised his stentorian voice above the din of the battle surrounding him and shouted: "Fire!" Up and down the Union line officers repeated his order, and the Union infantry responded.

On the right of the 14th Connecticut, the 1st Delaware and the 12th New Jersey regiments inflicted their share of casualties as Col. James K. Marshall and Brig. Gen. Joseph R. Davis struggled to bring their brigades up to the wall. But neither of these Federal regiments possessed the firepower of the 14th Connecticut. In addition to the eight companies of men shouldering Springfield rifles, two more companies, A and B, carried the new Sharps breechloaders, which were made in Connecticut. Soldiers trained to use this rifle worked in pairs, one loading while the other did the shooting. Sgt. Maj. Hincks recalled that "at that time I was firing two Sharps rifles, which Lieutenant Hawley [Lt. William H. Hawley of Bridgeport] was loading for me; they belonged to men wounded early in the day." A sharpshooter like Hincks could get shots off so quickly that the gun barrel became almost too hot to handle.[36]

As Fry's shattered regiments approached the corner of the outer wall, Garnett's brigade worked forward on his right. By this time Garnett's regiments had also lost unit cohesion; remnants of Kemper's brigade sifted through Garnett's lines. As Kemper turned to wave forward this wedged mass of infantry, he was killed. Getting under the range of Cushing's guns, these Confederate infantries succeeded in reaching the outside of the wall where they paused briefly before going up and over. Colonel Fry had succeeded in his mission to drive his brigade straight at the outer angle of the wall and to serve as the brigade of direction for the assault. Remnants of his right wing, the 1st Tennessee and 13th Alabama, prepared to go over the wall with what remained of Garnett's brigade. At that moment there was no Federal opposition on the other side of the outer wall, for Lt. Cushing was dead, his guns silent, and the 71st Pennsylvania had withdrawn in some disorder. Fry knew that one last strong, determined thrust could take these Confederates into the heart of the Union line.[37]

While the 1st Tennessee and 13th Alabama prepared to advance, the rest of Fry's brigade moved forward in support, closing in on that section of the wall protecting the 14th Connecticut. Sliding along the right side of the short wall connecting the outer and inner angles was the 14th Tennessee, and to the left of this unit were the 7th Tennessee and

5th Alabama, intent on reaching the Connecticut veterans on the reverse side of the piled-up stones. And they came close; they advanced sporadically, staying near the ground as their second and third lines worked forward amid their dead and wounded, while the Nutmeggers maintained a constant fire on their immediate front. Once beyond a line running parallel with the outer angle, the Confederates faced fire so withering that only the most daring continued up the slope.

On the immediate left of these regiments, Marshall's brigade worked its way toward that section of the wall defended by the 1st Delaware and 12th New Jersey, and remnants of Davis's brigade scrambled toward the corner of the wall that butted up against the Bryan house and barn. Caught in a cross-fire from behind the wall and along the lane on their left flank, the leading elements of Pettigrew's division were beaten into the ground directly in front of the 14th Connecticut. Here the 52d North Carolina "advanced under the incessant discharge of the cannon, assisted by the infantry's rifles, and had almost attained success, when by the overpowering force and almost impregnable position of the enemy . . . were forced back, and then the slaughter was terrific."[38]

Trimble had succeeded in getting his two brigades across the Emmitsburg Road in fair order. As Pettigrew's brigades seemed to bounce back from the wall, Trimble drove Lane's brigade to the support of the Confederate left flank, that corner of the field where Davis's brigade had disintegrated. At the same time Col. William Lowrance led his brigade straight at the 14th Connecticut and 1st Delaware regiments. When these 10 additional North Carolina regiments led by Lane and Lowrance swelled up toward the inner wall, the surge of Confederate power reached its high tide; if the inner wall were breached, the rush of Confederates would flood Cemetery Ridge. As the North Carolinians crashed their way forward, Brig. Gen. Lewis A. Armistead rallied the Southerners on their right flank.

Just to the left of the 14th Connecticut, Generals Hancock and Webb struggled to stem the ebb of the 71st Pennsylvania, as the remnants of that regiment had already retreated to ground to the left rear of the 14th Connecticut. Cushing's guns were silent. With the outer wall to the right of those guns undefended, Confederate battle flags began to pop up along that stone barrier. Once what remained of Garnett's brigade reached the wall, they stalled and took cover there; Armistead, marching behind Garnett, pressed forward with his Virginians. Passing through Garnett's broken regiments, Armistead leaped over the wall, and, with his hat stuck on the point of his sword, he waved frantically for his troops to follow him. And over the wall they came—hundreds of them.[39]

Smoke drifted and swirled above and along the battle line, making it difficult for Lee to see the breach his men had made in the Union center. But Hancock and his staff had no trouble seeing the danger, and they somehow managed to move forward the 72d Pennsylvania and two or three other regiments to plug the gap. Moreover, staff officers turned around the retreating elements of the 71st Pennsylvania and placed two companies of that regiment behind the inner wall to the immediate left of the 14th Connecticut.[40] With the help of additional regiments just south of the "clump of trees," Gibbon and Webb were able to box in the Confederates before they could gain much ground. And for the next 10 minutes, in an area no larger than a football field, came some of the most vicious hand-to-hand fighting of the Civil War.

In battle, infantrymen fighting for their lives are aware only of what is immediately before them. At Gettysburg this was true of the 14th Connecticut. When Armistead led his Confederates over the wall, he carried the fight to within 100 yards of the left flank of the Nutmeggers. But Major Ellis's men at that moment paid no attention to Armistead's advancing Confederates, for these Connecticut Yankees had enough trouble in their front. Lowrance's North Carolinians pushed towards them as Lane's brigade drove close to the men of the 12th New Jersey. But both Confederate commands found themselves hemmed in by the Union forces along the lane on their left flank, and they began being cut down by Hays's riflemen. Punished severely as they climbed the fences along the Emmitsburg Road, 38th North Carolina now constituted little more than a skirmish line; they came within a few feet of the wall but were able to advance no further.[41]

Indeed, the Confederates had come very close, and their heroic effort was now marked by the hundreds of dead and wounded men strewn across the slope from the Emmitsburg Road to the wall. Union colonel E. B. Cope, a veteran of the battle and later engineer of the Gettysburg Park Commission, reported after the war that "the dead were very numerous in the Angle around the spot where Armistead fell . . . but they were much more thickly strewn on the ground in front of the high stone wall which Pettigrew's and Trimble's men had tried to storm and which runs northward to the Bryan barn." The remaining Confederates now sought to surrender, or they turned back hoping to regain the safety of their own lines. The Nutmeggers claimed that "the Confederate line broke quicker in the immediate front of the Fourteenth than anywhere else." Because of Major Ellis's action once he felt certain that his front was secure, there is some evidence to support this claim. He noticed first that on his right the 12th New Jersey and 126th New York were containing General Lane's advance, but on his left Armistead's men were still pressing forward. Immediately Ellis shouted out: "Fourteenth, left oblique, fire!" The 1st Delaware followed the same order, and the effect was devastating. Combined with a renewed advance by the 72d Pennsylvania and other units, Armistead's command dissolved. And while a few managed to retreat, most were casualties.[42]

One of the last pockets of Confederate resistance contained some of the men of Lane's brigade. To the right of the 14th Connecticut where the wall sheltering the 12th New Jersey ended and the lane near the Bryan barn ran down toward the Emmitsburg Road, remnants of two or three regiments struggled to within a few feet of the wall protecting Hays's infantrymen. They had advanced as far as, if not beyond, the line reached by Armistead's men. (Years later North Carolina military historians would argue that Pettigrew's and Trimble's Confederates advanced farther and held their ground longer than anyone else along the line.) Hancock seemed to concur with these claims, for their persistence caused him enough concern to inform Meade at the end of the battle that he had "never seen a more formidable attack. . . . I had to break the line to attack the enemy in flank on my right, where the enemy was most persistent after the front attack was repelled. Not a rebel was in sight upright when I left. The line should be immediately restored and perfected." Lane led his North Carolinians up to the wall just to the right of the sector defended by the 14th Connecticut. His were the troops that concerned Hancock. Lane was one of only a few field commanders to escape the charge unhurt, and in his official report he noted that his men "advanced to within a few yards of the stone wall, exposed all the while to a heavy raking artillery fire from the right. My left was here very much exposed, and a column of the enemy's infantry was thrown forward in that direction, which enfiladed my whole line. This forced me to withdraw my brigade, the troops on my right having already done so."[43]

The Confederates on Lane's right were those facing the 14th Connecticut. The Nutmeggers had cleared their immediate front and were by that time directing their fire at a left oblique against Armistead's men. But not all of the men of the 14th participated; some jumped over the wall to seize Confederate regimental flags, whether lying on the ground or still clutched in the hands of wounded or dead color-bearers. Sergeant Major Hincks recalled that when he leaped over the wall the Confederates not in the act of surrendering "began to fall back as a mob—not all along or rapidly however. They still turned and fired and now and then made a brief stand." As Hincks raced for a Rebel standard, his ears caught the sound of whizzing bullets still flying through the air. He recalled that he jumped the wall near the inner angle where one of Arnold's guns had been abandoned. "In going after the flag, I ran past this gun, leaving it upon my left hand." Hincks captured the flag of the 14th Tennessee, and as his comrades cheered his return to the wall, four other Nutmeggers followed close behind him—all with captured colors.[44]

Major Ellis's men rounded up those Confederates strung out along their front; large numbers rose up and surrendered.

Among them was Capt. James M. Kincaid of Company G of the 52d North Carolina. Severely wounded, Kincaid was assisted by Cpl. Alexander McNeil of Company C, who recalled the meeting in a letter to a friend back in Waterbury written on 16 August 1863:

> I had a long conversation with a Captain of the 52nd North Carolina Regt. He was severely wounded and we carried him into our lines & laid him down. I gave him coffee to drink twice, while waiting for a stretcher to carry him to the Hospital. He was a sensible Intelligent man. He told me the South had been rough and harsh with North Carolina troops all through, since the War commenced. He told me that it was because the State of North Carolina did not *Secede* quite soon enough to suit some of the other Slave States. He told me, too, that the State of South Carolina ought to be sunk. That, he said, was where the trouble started.[45]

In his official report dated 6 July 1863, Major Ellis listed three Confederate regimental commanders who personally surrendered to him as they crossed over the wall: Col. John Fite, temporary commander of the 7th Tennessee; Lt. Col. N. J. George, commander of the 1st Tennessee; and Lt. Col. Marcus A. Parks, commander of the 52d North Carolina. Ellis then recorded the names of six more Confederate officers taken prisoner and added that "there were many of the Field and Line officers captured whose names could not be ascertained." Ellis also noted that "there came into the lines of this regiment about 100 or more of the enemy, some of whom were wounded, and gave themselves up."[46]

As the fighting ended on the northern end of Cemetery Ridge, the men there heard a new round of cannonading to the south. While no reserves had moved in behind General Armistead when he needed them, even as the survivors of Pickett's division struggled back to Seminary Ridge, two more Confederate brigades moved forward. Too late to assist Pickett, these men, under the command of General Wilcox, floundered forward and veered to the right, heading straight for McGilvery's guns. As Wilcox led his command across the Emmitsburg Road, Stannard's Vermonters did an about-face and prepared to flank Wilcox on the left. Along Colonel McGilvery's line, his artillerymen stared almost in disbelief at this new column of Confederates advancing, unsupported, toward them. Sterling's battery joined the others in a concentrated bombardment that tore great gaps in the hapless Confederates. A bewildered General Wilcox put it this way: "Here they were exposed to a close and terrible fire of artillery. Two lines of the enemy's infantry were seen moving by the flank to the rear of my left. . . . Knowing that my small force could do nothing save to make a useless sacrifice of themselves, I ordered them back. The enemy did not pursue."[47]

Union forces did not pursue; instead they were content to gather prisoners. Many of Wilcox's Alabamans and Floridians realized that it was useless to try to overrun the guns facing them. A few in the forward lines simply dropped to the ground intent on surrender; others managed to return to their original positions. Sterling did not note that his men took any prisoners, but they joined in the elation and shouts of triumph that now carried up and down Cemetery Ridge. This had been their first serious engagement with the Confederates, and they had performed like veterans. When Captain Sterling checked the condition of his battery at the close of the battle, he discovered that his losses were light—only three slightly wounded men, three dead horses, and one limber chest.[48]

Up on the ridge to the right of Sterling's battery, the joy was great among the men of the 14th Connecticut and all those in Hays's division. As his regiments collected prisoners by the hundreds, brought in the wounded, and piled up captured Confederate battle flags in front of his headquarters, Hays, always the dramatic leader, leaped onto his horse, seized two captured flags, and rode along the front of the wall. Amid shouts of victory from the men of his command, Hays approached the wall connecting the inner and outer angles, guided his horse across the front of the 14th Connecticut, and then paraded directly to the rear of the men still dragging flags behind him. So great was the noise and visible commotion that General Lee and his staff became aware of it and surmised that Meade had arrived on that part of the field to accept the acclaim of his soldiers. Indeed Meade had ridden forward just as the battle around "the little clump of trees" reached its climax, but the story goes that he managed to restrain his emotions, waving his hand just once or twice and singing out "Hurrah!" Meanwhile, across the field, Gen. Robert E. Lee had moved forward to greet and comfort his troops. He assumed full responsibility for the defeat, and to the small bands of returning Southerners he repeated again and again, "It was all my fault."[49]

As the celebration along the Union line subsided, the men of the 14th turned their attention to the many horrors in front of them. Chaplain Henry S. Stevens of Cromwell later recalled the scene: "Poor wounded wretches, scattered or lying in heaps, over the fields and in the road far in front, were writhing in agonies or straightening out in the last death shiver. Some unhurt ones who dared were running with all their might to reach their own lines."[50] Checking the condition of his own men, Major Ellis was amazed to discover that only one man had been killed and two wounded during the entire assault. The wall had proved a most effective shield for his men. After looking to the needs of his wounded and those of other Union regiments nearby, Ellis released some of his men to gather Confederate wounded. Among those men detailed for this duty was Pvt. Joseph L. Pierce of Berlin, a member of Company F. Known as "the only Chinaman in the Army of the Potomac," Pierce could be readily distinguished from other men in the company by the long pigtail he wore down his back. Born in China in 1842, Pierce was picked up as an orphan in Japan by a ship's master from New Britain, Capt. Joseph A. Pierce, who brought him home and adopted him. His adopted son did Captain Pierce great honor at Gettysburg, being among the first to go out on the skirmish line on 2 July and volunteering for the attack against the Bliss farm on 3 July.[51]

As Pierce and his comrades worked to bring in the Confederate wounded, the slanting rays of the setting sun filtered through the woods along Seminary Ridge, and the whole battlefield softened into twilight. Skirmishers from both armies once more worked their way forward from the main lines while their comrades along each ridge regrouped for the night. But it was a restless evening for many of the men, who battled fatigue and hunger and listened to the plaintive cries for help from the wounded not yet brought in. Pvt. Loren H. Goodrich of New Britain, a comrade of Private Pierce in the same company, noted in a letter to a friend that hunger more than compassion initially drove him over the stone wall to search the Confederate dead and wounded for food (the unit's rations had run out the previous evening). While he found "a plenty of fresh meat and wheat bread" in the haversacks he gathered, he felt considerable guilt and was deeply moved at the pathos of the scene.

> It was a horrible sight to see those poor fellows lying there who a few hours before were in the full bloom of manhood. One man who lived 2 hours after the battle was holding in his hand the picture of his wife and children. There he died with no loving hand or kind friend to soothe or cheer him with kind words, grasping in his death clutch the picture of those inocent ones who will be left fatherless. I passed on to another man, touched him to see if he was alive. He looked up; the stamp of death was marked on his features. Says he: "young freind give me a drink of water." He would not raise his head to drink. One of my companions being with me raised his head for him which was covered with blood. I had a canteen which holds 3 pints of water that I gave to him. He drank the whole of it and he wanted more. The night was still and dark; I could hear the groans of the wounded that lay betwixst the two skirmish lines nearly a half a mile off calling for water.[52]

The 14th Connecticut spent the night behind the same walls it had defended that day. A morning rain on 4 July added to the miseries of the untended wounded, and it did little to ease the efforts of fatigued veterans seeking a few hours rest.

Fully anticipating the possibility of another day of fighting, the Nutmeggers did not yet know that the Confederates along Seminary Ridge and Culp's Hill were preparing to break contact and withdraw. Lee had conceded that he no longer had the strength to shake Meade loose from Cemetery Ridge and that he now wished to withdraw his army to Virginia.

# "They Felt the Shock of Battle"

# 7

# The Aftermath

---

The men who fought there were the tried fighters,
The hammered, the weather-beaten, the very hard
    dying men.
            —Stephen Vincent Benét, *John Brown's Body*

AS LEE WITHDREW from Gettysburg's blood-soaked fields, many hard-dying men in blue and gray remained in the muddy fields and along the rocky ledges of Culp's Hill, the Round Tops, Devil's Den, and Cemetery Ridge. Lee had gambled on a thrust toward Harrisburg, but Meade had called his hand. Years later John B. Gordon phrased it succinctly: "Victory to Lee meant Southern independence. Victory to Meade meant an inseparable Union. The life of the Confederacy, the unity of the Republic—these were the stakes of July 3."[1]

By late morning of 4 July, Meade knew that Lee had withdrawn from Gettysburg. Union patrols confirmed that the Confederates had already vacated the town, and the rear guard regiments were shielding roads leading west to the mountain gaps, the retreat route of the Confederates. Two Connecticut regiments were among the first to learn that Gettysburg had been evacuated and report the news to Meade. On the morning of 4 July, the 17th Connecticut was issued orders by General Ames to send out a skirmish line "into the meadows at the foot of East Cemetery Hill, and to proceed toward the town, feeling for the enemy." Meanwhile, there had been a change in command of the 17th; Major Brady was relieved by Col. William H. Noble, who rejoined the unit on the night of 3 July. He selected Lt. Milton H.

Daniels of Company C to lead the skirmishing party. As soon as it was light enough to see a few feet through the rising mist, Daniels moved his detail into the meadow east of Cemetery Hill and eased toward the town. Because of low visibility, Daniels cautioned his men to stay within sight of each other and issued commands by hand signals only as his men crept toward the area recently controlled by the Louisiana Tigers and Colonel Avery's North Carolinians. It was ticklish work. Sgt. Patrick Wade of Company K, a native of Bridgeport, remembered later how the detail moved gingerly across the meadow, "going forward about 100 feet and then lying flat on our faces and listening, trying to hear some sound from the enemy. Then we would advance again."[2]

Gradually, the skirmishers worked their way to the edge of town, surprised and pleased to find the outskirts clear of Confederates. Moving into town, they noticed a few men in the mist and pale light of morning. Then an officer appeared wildly waving his hat and beckoning the skirmishers forward; he proved to be a Union officer released by the Confederates just hours earlier. He reported to Daniels that Lee's army had pulled clear of the town at about three o'clock that morning and appeared to be in full retreat. Daniels immediately sent word to General Ames, and within minutes Colonel Noble moved forward to secure the town.

As the news of Lee's withdrawal spread among the Union troops, another Connecticut regiment was closing in on the town. Roused from sodden blankets, Colonel Packer's 5th Connecticut joined a probe led personally by General Slocum. They were to scout the area east of Gettysburg, where on the previous day General Stuart had led an unsuccessful attack against Union cavalry. This was to be a reconnaissance in force, and the command included the 5th Connecticut, 123d New York, 46th Pennsylvania from Colonel McDougall's First Brigade of the First Division, and Colonel Colgrove's regiments of the Third Brigade. Augmented by an artillery battery, these regiments moved forward at 7:00 A.M.[3]

Confederates were nowhere in evidence in the fields to the east and northeast of Culp's Hill. Certain that Stuart had withdrawn, Slocum turned his command toward Gettysburg and moved into the terrain previously occupied by General Johnson's division of Ewell's corps. The area was clear; not even a rear guard action slowed their advance.

Of the five Connecticut regiments at Gettysburg, Colonel Packer's 5th Connecticut saw the least action. By chance, that brigade seldom came into contact with the Confederates during the entire fight. The regiment suffered only minor casualties, and Packer had trouble finding episodes for his official report that would enhance the image of his troops. He did, however, stake out one claim coincident with the regiment's participation in General Slocum's foray. Packer recorded that when they turned toward town, his regiment "marched completely around our right flank; also in front of our line of battle, being the first regiment of infantry to pass through the town of Gettysburg."[4] By late morning the 5th Connecticut had completed its reconnaissance and returned to Culp's Hill to rejoin the brigade.

With the news of the Confederate retreat, the rejoicing was great all along the Union lines. As one veteran of the 5th Connecticut phrased it, "we are celebrating our first victory. The enemy has retreated, the victory is ours, and our forces are in possession of the entire field." Then, as an afterthought, he wrote, "special details engaged in burying the dead." Chaplain Stevens of the 14th Connecticut noted that the rejoicing of the men in his regiment was tempered by the unpleasant duty of burying the dead of both sides, "in some places so numerous that the ground appeared covered by them, and one could walk for distances stepping only on the bodies of the slain."[5] All along the Union position soldiers buried the dead, collected scattered arms and ammunition, tended to wounded comrades, and wondered how soon Meade would follow up on his great victory by ordering a pursuit. But the command was long in coming, too long in the opinion of many. A wary and cautious Meade first ordered his cavalry to probe the areas west of Gettysburg and to harass the Confederates wherever possible. Then, on 5 July, General Sedgwick moved the Sixth Corps from Little Round Top toward the Hagerstown Road, getting the pursuit underway. By the next day the remainder of the army was on the move. But by now Lee had reached the vicinity of Williamsport on the banks of the Potomac River, and safety was just a short distance farther across the river.

All five Connecticut regiments eventually moved out with the Army of the Potomac, but as the campaign concluded with Lee's escape across the river, the Nutmeg regiments went their separate ways for the remainder of the war. Only the 14th Connecticut remained with the Army of the Potomac for the duration of the conflict, and when the Second Corps of that army pressed forward toward Appomattox, the colors of the "Fighting Fourteenth" waved proudly over these men from Connecticut. Of all the regiments from the state, the 14th was "in the greatest number of battles . . . and lost the largest percentage of men in killed, wounded and died in the service."[6]

After Gettysburg, the 5th and 20th Connecticut, still brigaded in the Twelfth Corps, followed Lee's army to Virginia. Then in September they moved west to Chattanooga to join the Army of the Cumberland. In April 1864 the 11th and 12th Corps were combined to form the 20th Corps, which later that year joined Sherman on his "March to the Sea."[7]

The 17th Connecticut was assigned to the Southern Department in August 1863 and was first sent to Folly Island, near Charleston, to participate in the Union operations against the city's defenses—notably the siege of Battery Wagner. In February 1864 the unit was transferred to Florida and headquartered at St. Augustine, and for the duration of the conflict these men protected that area of the state against Confederate raids on Union installations.[8]

When the 27th Connecticut came down from the hills of Gettysburg, it had just 35 effectives. Along with Caldwell's division of the Second Corps, this small contingent arrived near Williamsport on the Potomac River "in time to participate in the closing scenes of an engagement resulting in the capture of the enemy's rear guard, more than one thousand strong." On 18 July the veterans of the 27th were released and returned to New Haven, where they arrived on 22 July "greeted by every token of enthusiastic and hospitable welcome that the military companies, municipal authorities, and loyal populace of New Haven could bestow."⁹

Connecticut's only artillery battery at Gettysburg left the field on 5 July with the Artillery Reserve and a few days later resumed its defense of Washington. Then on 22 August the battery was sent to New York City to assist in ending the tragic Draft Riots. After that unpleasant assignment, Captain Sterling's men moved south again, this time assigned to the Department of the Gulf, occupying positions near New Orleans and Mobile. On 9 August 1865 the unit returned to Connecticut to be mustered out in New Haven.¹⁰

By late summer 1865, most of Connecticut's veterans had come home, content with the thought that they had helped preserve the Union. Once the roar of cannons and the flight of bullets had ceased, these veterans began the struggle of adjusting to life in peacetime and returning to civilian occupations. But as time passed, the memory of their struggles drew Connecticut veterans back to the fields where once they had bled and watched their comrades die; men from the Nutmeg State were among the first to erect memorials on the Gettysburg Battlefield.¹¹

In July 1884 survivors of the 14th and 17th Connecticut made their first trip back since the war to erect monuments at Cemetery Ridge and Barlow's Knoll. This time the men were cheerful and the occasion festive. For while the passing of more than 20 years had not erased all the pain and sorrow, the men looked to the future, hoping their families and friends would learn and benefit from their sacrifices. These veterans were greeted warmly by the residents of Gettysburg, with most of the local arrangements handled by Gettysburg's Post 9 of the Grand Army of the Republic, which opened its hall on East Middle Street for the occasion. Recognizing the importance of the visit of these veterans to the town's rapidly developing tourist trade, the *Gettysburg Compiler* described on 8 July the events of the previous week, including the 17th Connecticut dedication ceremony on 1 July.

Tuesday morning a procession composed of survivors of the 17th Connecticut with the New Oxford Band, members of other regiments with the Warwick Band, G.A.R. and citizens marched to the monument on Barlow's Knoll, north of the Almshouse. The covering surrounding the monument was removed by two Connecticut ladies, one the daughter of a soldier killed on this spot. Chaplain W. K. Hall opened with prayer and was followed by Hon. P. C. Lounsbury with an oration well fitting the occasion. Addresses of presentation and acceptance were made by Lt. Col. Henry Allen, Gen. W. H. Noble and D. A. Buehler, Esq., V.P. of the Memorial Association. The monument, as described last week, is of Connecticut granite, appropriately inscribed, and presents an imposing appearance.

As also noted by the *Compiler*, 100 veterans of the 14th arrived on 1 July, and that evening "many of the visiting comrades met members of G.A.R. Post 9 at their hall, and several hours were pleasantly spent." The next evening "a lively 'camp-fire' took place on the avenue at the 14th Connecticut monument," with speeches and songs making up the program. Then at three o'clock on Thursday, 3 July, the unit dedicated its "massive Gettysburg granite monument, built by J. W. Flaharty of Gettysburg." Chaplain Henry Stevens of Cromwell gave the oration, followed by brief remarks by Col. Samuel Moore of New Britain and Sgt. Benjamin Hirst of Vernon. During his oration, Chaplain Stevens told his audience:

You place here where you stood, by battle's tide begirt, on Gettysburg's immortal day, your historic and symbolic monument, purchased largely by the contributions of you who are poor, and poor because you gave your best days and strength to save your nation from disruption. Your stone is not mortuary, but historic; not reared in honor of only those who fell here or fought here, but to commemorate the regiment and its history as a whole. Its granite substance felt the shock of the battle which you helped make a victory for the Union, and its base will hold for you through ages the position you held . . . [12]

And so the veterans continued to come, and by the fall of 1889 every unit had placed at least one monument on the field. The last big gathering of Connecticut veterans took place in 1913 during the fiftieth anniversary of the battle, when nearly 50,000 Union and Confederate veterans gathered for the "Grand Reunion." Writing of that event, Charles F. Hallock of Norwalk, formerly a member of Company E of the 5th Connecticut, summarized the feelings of all his comrades when he noted that "we got along very well not having forgotten how we had to get along when we were in this vicinity in 1863." He concluded by saying that "after having one grand time we left the great Camp . . . and arrived back Home in good old Connecticut feeling glad that we had again been permitted to visit the Battle Field."[13] That same summer, in June, another Connecticut delegation came to Little Round Top to dedicate an equestrian statue of Maj. Gen. John Sedgwick. In accepting the monument from Connecticut on behalf of the federal government, Assistant Secretary of War Henry Breckinridge voiced the sentiments of the Connecticut veterans when he observed:

Woe be to the nation that forgets her heroes. Keep green the memory of our martyrs; teach the children the great deeds of their forebears; kindle the torch of patriotism with the fire of zeal and devotion. Hold to the things that are good. Preserve the simplicity and liberty of our political life and, under God, our country will survive the centuries in an ever continuing increase of greatness and justice.[14]

# APPENDIX:

# CONNECTICUT CASUALTIES AT

# GETTYSBURG

CASUALTIES AT GETTYSBURG were high. While historians differ as to the exact strength of both armies during the battle, the most recent scholarship on the subject suggests that Meade's Army of the Potomac went into the fight with 93,540 men while Lee's Army of Northern Virginia went to the battle with 69,915.[1] After Gettysburg, Lee's army had been reduced by 22,587 men, about 32 percent, while Meade's losses numbered 23,049, about 25 percent.[2]

The percentage of Connecticut casualties was slightly higher than that of the Army of the Potomac as a whole. The Nutmeg State fielded 1,285 officers and men during the battle and lost 359 in killed, wounded, captures, or missing, 28 percent of its strength. The lists compiled here were based on the rosters contained in *Record of Service of Connecticut Men in the Army and Navy of the United States during the War of the Rebellion* and John W. Busey's *These Honored Dead: The Union Casualties at Gettysburg.*

Of the 75 men killed or mortally wounded at Gettysburg, 19 are buried in the Connecticut section of the National Cemetery, two in the adjoining Evergreen Cemetery, and three other soldiers were mistakenly buried in the Connecticut section of the National Cemetery (these 21 indicated with asterisks). Rosters of the Connecticut units carry no records for William Cannells, S. Carter, and a soldier whose last name was Williams, supposedly of Company D, 20th Regiment. In the listings that follow, asterisks appear next to the names of those soldiers buried at Gettysburg; a separate list of

[1] These figures are derived from John W. Busey and David G. Martin, *Regimental Strengths at Gettysburg*, 12, 129.

[2] See Robert K. Krick, *The Gettysburg Death Roster: The Confederate Dead at Gettysburg*, 17; and John W. Busey, *These Honored Dead: The Union Casualties at Gettysburg*, 6.

them is also appended. Concluding this section of the appendix is a partial list of Connecticut natives who were casualties while fighting with other units.

## TABULATION OF CONNECTICUT CASUALTIES

| Regiments | 5th | 14th | 17th | 20th | 27th | Total |
|---|---|---|---|---|---|---|
| Killed or Mortally Wounded | 0 | 14 | 34 | 8 | 12 | 68 |
| Wounded | 3 | 49 | 79 | 28 | 21 | 180 |
| Captured | 7 | 4 | 77 | 0 | 3 | 91 |
| Wounded and Captured | 0 | 1 | 10 | 0 | 2 | 13 |
| Missing in Action | 0 | 0 | 6 | 0 | 1 | 7 |
| Total | 10 | 68 | 206 | 36 | 39 | 359 |

## CONNECTICUT REGIMENTAL CASUALTIES AT GETTYSBURG
### Killed or Mortally Wounded

| Name | Rank | Regiment | Residence | Date of Death |
|---|---|---|---|---|
| Ames, Thomas M. | Corporal | 14th | Waterford | 3 July |
| Baldwin, George W. | Sergeant | 14th | Middlebury | 14 July |
| Barnum, Bethel S. | Sergeant | 17th | Bethel | 1 July |
| *Benson, Frank J. | Private | 17th | Brookfield | 17 July |
| Black, John A. | Private | 17th | Bridgeport | 1 July |
| Blackman, Theodore | Private | 17th | Bethel | 2 July |
| Bodwell, William | Private | 27th | Norwalk | 5 July |
| Booth, John R. | Private | 17th | Stratford | 1 July |
| Brainard, Thomas J. | Private | 14th | Bloomfield | 3 July |
| Bradley, William F. | Private | 17th | Monroe | 1 July |
| Britto, Sylvester | Private | 17th | Wilton | 4 July |
| Bronson, Augustus | Sergeant | 17th | Danbury | 5 July |
| Burns, Henry | Corporal | 17th | Norwalk | 1 July |
| Carney, Lawrence | Private | 17th | Ridgefield | 1 July |
| *Cassidy, James | Private | 20th | Hartford | 13 July |
| Chapman, Jedediah | Captain | 27th | New Haven | 2 July |
| *Clark, Aaron A. | Private | 14th | Haddam | 3 July |
| *Clement, Moses G. | Private | 14th | Guilford | 3 July |
| Comstock, Samuel | Sergeant | 17th | New Canaan | 27 Sept. |
| *Confrey, Michael | Private | 27th | New Haven | 2 July |
| Cornwall, Charles | Corporal | 27th | Milford | 2 July |
| Crabbe, Cassius M. | Private | 17th | Bridgeport | 1 July |
| Crofut, Stephen C. | Private | 17th | Stratford | 1 July |

## Killed or Mortally Wounded (continued)

| Name | Rank | Regiment | Residence | Date of Death |
|------|------|----------|-----------|---------------|
| Dauchy, William O. | 1st Sergeant | 17th | Danbury | 1 July |
| Delevan, Smith | Private | 17th | Danbury | 15 July |
| *Dibble, Alfred H. | Private | 14th | Westbrook | 5 July |
| *Dickerman, Joel C. | Corporal | 20th | Hamden | 3 July |
| *Dunn, Patrick | Private | 27th | Wallingford | 2 July |
| *Farr, Edward B. | Private | 27th | New Haven | 2 July |
| *Flynn, James | Private | 17th | Westport | 14 July |
| Foot, Francis | Private | 17th | Westport | 1 July |
| Fowler, Douglas | Lt. Colonel | 17th | Norwalk | 1 July |
| Fox, Michael | Private | 17th | Stamford | 1 July |
| Goodell, William | Corporal | 14th | Vernon | 3 July |
| Goodwin, John | Private | 27th | New Haven | 2 July |
| Gordon, James | Sergeant | 17th | Newtown | 1 July |
| Gregory, William S. | Private | 17th | Greenwich | 1 July |
| Guernsey, George H. | Private | 17th | Westport | 9 Aug. |
| Hill, Albert M. | Private | 14th | Westbrook | 29 July |
| *Hodge, Nelson | Private | 14th | Coventry | 25 July |
| Huxham, Samuel | Corporal | 14th | Middletown | 3 July |
| Judson, Marcus O. | Private | 27th | New Haven | 2 July |
| Julian, John F. | Private | 14th | Vernon | 6 July |
| *Marsh, William D. | Private | 14th | Madison | 3 July |
| Mead, Eliphalet | Private | 17th | New Canaan | 1 July |
| Merwin, Henry C. | Lt. Colonel | 27th | New Haven | 2 July |
| *Metcalf, John W. | Private | 17th | Norwalk | 2 July |
| Moore, James E. | Captain | 17th | Danbury | 1 July |
| Morgan, Wilber B. | Private | 17th | Wilton | 16 Aug. |
| *Mulvey, Bernard | Private | 20th | Hamden | 3 July |
| Nash, Francis | Private | 17th | Westport | 1 July |
| Pickett, Edwin D. | 1st Sergeant | 17th | Ridgefield | 1 July |
| *Perry, John D. | Private | 20th | New Haven | 3 July |
| *Puffer, Joseph | Corporal | 14th | Coventry | 3 July |
| *Purdy, Daniel | Private | 17th | Danbury | 15 July |
| Redshaw, Thomas | Private | 20th | Derby | 3 July |
| Roberts, Charles F. | Private | 20th | Hartford | 3 July |
| *Roberts, Charles H. | Private | 20th | Newtown | 9 July |
| Scott, William O. | Private | 27th | Milford | 2 July |
| Simons, Thomas | Sergeant | 20th | Cheshire | 23 July |
| Standish, Walter F. | Corporal | 14th | Sprague | 3 July |
| Taylor, Richard D. | Private | 17th | Danbury | 2 July |
| Warren, Rufus | Private | 17th | Ridgefield | 1 July |
| Westlake, William W. | Corporal | 17th | Norwalk | 2 July |
| *Whitlock, Joseph S. | Private | 17th | Ridgefield | 1 July |
| *Wilcox, Alva E. | Corporal | 17th | Bridgeport | 6 July |
| *Wilson, William E. | Corporal | 27th | New Haven | 2 July |
| Yale, Thomas G. | Private | 27th | New Haven | 26 Aug. |

## Wounded

| Name | Rank | Regiment | Residence | Date |
|------|------|----------|-----------|------|
| Abbott, Nathan D. | Sergeant | 20th | Watertown | 3 July |
| Allen, Bradley | Private | 20th | Hamden | 3 July |
| Allen, Henry | Captain | 17th | Norwalk | 3 July |
| Ames, Fisher A. | Private | 20th | New Haven | 3 July |
| Bailey, Samuel M. | Private | 20th | Southington | 3 July |
| Barber, George W. | Private | 17th | Danbury | 1 July |
| Barrows, Isaac C. | Private | 14th | Vernon | 3 July |
| Bebo, Frank | Private | 14th | Putnam | 3 July |
| Benedict, John H. | Corporal | 17th | Danbury | 1 July |
| Benham, James W. | Private | 14th | Middlebury | 3 July |
| Bennett, Abner F. | Private | 17th | Fairfield | 1 July |
| Blakeman, J. Henry | Private | 17th | Stratford | 1 July |
| Bouton, John W. | Private | 17th | Danbury | 1 July |
| Bradley, Joseph R. | Captain | 27th | East Haven | 2 July |
| Brady, Allen G. | Major | 17th | Torrington | 2 July |
| Brennan, Cornelius | Private | 14th | Norwich | 3 July |
| Brigham, George N. | Sergeant | 14th | Vernon | 3 July |
| Brockett, Dwight T. | Private | 27th | New Haven | 2 July |
| Bronson, Harvey R. | Private | 20th | Derby | 3 July |
| Brooks, Thomas H. | Private | 20th | Bethany | 3 July |
| Brown, John | Private | 20th | New Britain | 3 July |
| Buckley, Patrick | Private | 17th | Norwalk | 1 July |
| Bulger, John | Private | 17th | Norwalk | - July |
| Burtis, Warren J. | Private | 17th | Bridgeport | 1 July |
| Byington, Theodore D. | Corporal | 14th | Waterbury | 3 July |
| Carpenter, Frederick H. | Corporal | 17th | Bridgeport | 1 July |
| Chaffee, Sanford E. | Captain | 20th | Derby | 2 July |
| Chapman, Stanley L. | Corporal | 14th | Westbrook | 3 July |
| Clark, Henry W. | Corporal | 27th | New Haven | 2 July |
| Clark, Michael | Private | 17th | Greenwich | 1 July |
| Coit, James B. | Captain | 14th | Norwich | 3 July |
| Collins, John | Private | 17th | Stamford | 1 July |
| Cooper, Peter | Private | 14th | Hartford | 3 July |
| Corkins, William | Corporal | 20th | Hartford | 2 July |
| Critenton, Thomas L. | Private | 14th | Hartford | 3 July |
| Culver, Warren | Private | 20th | East Haddam | 3 July |
| Cutts, William H. | Private | 20th | Southbury | 3 July |
| Dailey, Patrick | Private | 14th | Middletown | 3 July |
| Daley, Cornelius | Private | 14th | Middletown | 3 July |
| Davis, Danford J. | Private | 14th | Berlin | 3 July |
| Dayton, John S. | Corporal | 17th | Darien | 1 July |
| DeForrest, Henry W. | Private | 17th | Bridgeport | 1 July |
| DeForrest, Samuel C. | Private | 17th | Wilton | 1 July |
| Dennis, James | Private | 17th | Bridgeport | 3 July |
| Dennis, John H. | Private | 17th | Westport | 2 July |

## Wounded (continued)

| Name | Rank | Regiment | Residence | Date |
|------|------|----------|-----------|------|
| Dewhirst, William B. | Private | 17th | Bridgeport | 1 July |
| Dickinson, George | Sergeant | 20th | Hartford | 3 July |
| Dixon, Levi | Private | 17th | New Canaan | 1 July |
| Donelson, John W. | Corporal | 5th | New Britain | 2 July |
| Downing, John | Private | 20th | Portland | 3 July |
| Dubois, Cornelius J. | Captain | 27th | New Haven | 2 July |
| Eagon, Dennis | 1st Sergeant | 17th | Greenwich | 1 July |
| Edwards, Thaddeus | Private | 17th | Bethel | 1 July |
| Ely, Edgar S. | Private | 14th | Madison | 3 July |
| Fahey, John H. | Private | 20th | Hamden | 3 July |
| Feeks, Thaddeus | Private | 17th | Danbury | 3 July |
| Ferry, Francis H. | Private | 17th | Bethel | 1 July |
| Finn, Thomas | Private | 14th | New Britain | 3 July |
| Fitzpatrick, John | Private | 17th | Stamford | 2 July |
| Foley, John H. | Sergeant | 17th | Bridgeport | 1 July |
| Ford, Gilbert A. W. | Corporal | 27th | New Haven | 2 July |
| Fowler, Edward | Corporal | 5th | Groton | 3 July |
| Fowler, Edward B. | Private | 27th | East Haven | 2 July |
| Fox, Hiram H. | Private | 14th | Middletown | 3 July |
| Fox, John | Private | 14th | Bridgeport | 3 July |
| Frankenfield, Henry H. | Corporal | 14th | Hartford | 3 July |
| Frisbee, Henry R. | Private | 14th | Middletown | 3 July |
| Gardner, Thomas W. | Corporal | 14th | Waterford | 3 July |
| Gibbon, John | Private | 20th | Cheshire | 3 July |
| Gibson, Charles H. | Corporal | 20th | Portland | 3 July |
| Gilbert, Isaac W. | Private | 17th | Norwalk | 2 July |
| Glenn, Russell | Corporal | 14th | Bridgeport | 3 July |
| Grace, William | Private | 17th | Norwalk | 2 July |
| Griffin, John | Private | 27th | New Haven | 2 July |
| Grynan, James | Private | 14th | New London | 3 July |
| Guild, Augustus | Private | 14th | Middletown | 3 July |
| Hagar, Abijah | Private | 17th | Wilton | 2 July |
| Hale, George | Corporal | 17th | Westport | 2 July |
| Hall, Chauncey | Corporal | 20th | Cheshire | 3 July |
| Hannaford, George W. | Private | 17th | Bridgeport | 1 July |
| Harrington, John H. | Private | 17th | Ridgefield | 1 July |
| Hayes, George R. | Private | 17th | Bridgeport | 1 July |
| Hayes, John L. | Private | 17th | Norwalk | 2 July |
| Held, J. Henry, Jr. | Sergeant | 17th | Greenwich | 1 July |
| Henderson, Charles H. | Private | 27th | New Haven | 2 July |
| Hirst, Benjamin | Sergeant | 14th | Vernon | 3 July |
| Hobbie, Selah R. | Corporal | 17th | Stamford | 1 July |
| Hubbard, George A. | Sergeant | 14th | Middletown | 3 July |
| Jackson, William H. | Private | 17th | Stamford | 1 July |
| Keeler, Henry W. | Sergeant | 17th | New Haven | 1 July |

## Wounded (continued)

| Name | Rank | Regiment | Residence | Date |
|------|------|----------|-----------|------|
| King, Miles | Private | 20th | Hartford | 3 July |
| Knowlton, Julius W. | Sergeant | 14th | Bridgeport | 3 July |
| Kohlrissen, Theodore | Private | 14th | New London | 3 July |
| Lee, Aaron W. | Corporal | 17th | Ridgefield | 1 July |
| Lees, Edward M. | 2d Lieutenant | 17th | Westport | 1 July |
| Lentz, Joseph | Private | 20th | Cheshire | 3 July |
| Light, David | Private | 17th | Greenwich | 1 July |
| Lindhein, Frederick | Private | 17th | Bridgeport | 1 July |
| Lucas, Walter M. | Captain | 14th | Middletown | 2 July |
| Lungwitz, Valentine | Private | 14th | Waterbury | 3 July |
| McAuley, William J. | Private | 20th | New Haven | 3 July |
| McCuen, Owen | Private | 14th | Waterbury | 3 July |
| McDermott, Michael | Private | 14th | Killingly | 3 July |
| McDonough, Henry | Sergeant | 17th | Westport | 2 July |
| McElroy, Charles | Private | 17th | Bridgeport | 2 July |
| McHugh, John | Private | 17th | Danbury | 1 July |
| McKay, Fred A. | Corporal | 17th | Fairfield | 2 July |
| McVay, Francis | Private | 14th | Norwich | 3 July |
| Marsh, Thomas A. | Private | 17th | Easton | 1 July |
| Marshall, Barney | Private | 17th | Trumbull | 1 July |
| Merrill, Martin | Private | 27th | Orange | 2 July |
| Mills, William E. | Private | 17th | Darien | 3 July |
| Montieth, James | Private | 17th | Westport | 2 July |
| Morrison, Charles F. | Private | 14th | Willington | 3 July |
| Murray, Edward J. | Sergeant | 20th | New Britain | 3 July |
| Newton, James | Private | 17th | Bridgeport | 1 July |
| Nichols, Charles H. | Private | 27th | New Haven | 2 July |
| Northrop, William H. | Private | 17th | Darien | 1 July |
| Northrup, Seth A. | Private | 17th | Norwalk | 1 July |
| O'Connell, Michael | Private | 14th | New Britain | 3 July |
| O'Doharty, Philip | Private | 17th | Greenwich | 1 July |
| O'Neal, Daniel | Private | 27th | New Haven | 2 July |
| Paden, Charles | Private | 27th | Wallingford | 2 July |
| Patrick, William | Private | 14th | Waterbury | 3 July |
| Peck, Aaron | Private | 17th | Redding | 1 July |
| Perry, Robert N. | Private | 17th | Norwalk | 2 July |
| Peterson, George F. | Adjutant | 27th | New Haven | 2 July |
| Phillips, John | Private | 27th | New Haven | 2 July |
| Price, John | Private | 20th | Hartford | 3 July |
| Prince, Charles P. | 1st Lieutenant | 27th | East Haven | 2 July |
| Purdy, Patrick | Private | 17th | Norwalk | 2 July |
| Quien, Henry | 2d Lieutenant | 17th | Danbury | 2 July |
| Rice, William A. | Private | 14th | Waterbury | 3 July |
| Riley, James | Private | 14th | Middletown | 3 July |
| Rockwell, Darius B. | Corporal | 17th | Wilton | 2 July |

## Wounded (continued)

| Name | Rank | Regiment | Residence | Date |
|------|------|----------|-----------|------|
| Rounds, Sylvester | Private | 17th | Huntington | 1 July |
| Royston, James | Private | 20th | New Britain | 3 July |
| Sage, James H. | Private | 14th | Middletown | 3 July |
| Schmidt, Peter | Private | 27th | New Haven | 3 July |
| Scofield, Andrew | Private | 17th | New Canaan | 2 July |
| Scranton, Alonzo | Private | 17th | Bridgeport | 1 July |
| Searles, Mortimer | Private | 17th | Stamford | 1 July |
| Seercy, John | Private | 17th | Fairfield | 2 July |
| Selleck, Benjamin | Private | 17th | Darien | 1 July |
| Seward, Samuel H. | 2d Lieutenant | 14th | Waterbury | 3 July |
| Seymour, Frederick S. | 1st Lieutenant | 14th | New Britain | 3 July |
| Shalk, Frederick E. | 2d Lieutenant | 14th | Norwich | 3 July |
| Silliman, Justus M. | Private | 17th | New Canaan | 1 July |
| Smith, William D. | Private | 14th | Middletown | 3 July |
| Smith, William H. | Private | 17th | Bethel | 3 July |
| Snagg, Henry L. | Sergeant Major | 14th | Waterbury | 3 July |
| Stafford, Albert | Private | 5th | Plainfield | 2 July |
| Stannard, John S. | Corporal | 14th | Guilford | 3 July |
| Stannis, William H. | Corporal | 27th | Meriden | 2 July |
| Stevens, John B. | Private | 14th | Madison | 3 July |
| Still, Jacob L. | Private | 20th | Seymour | 3 July |
| Stoughton, Frank E. | 2d Lieutenant | 14th | Vernon | 3 July |
| Swank, George T. | 1st Sergeant | 27th | New Haven | 2 July |
| Swords, Alfred | Private | 17th | Norwalk | 1 July |
| Tenner, Richard A. | Private | 27th | New Haven | 2 July |
| Thompson, Henry | Private | 17th | Huntington | 1 July |
| Thorp, Samuel | Sergeant | 17th | Bridgeport | 1 July |
| Tibitts, John A. | 2d Lieutenant | 14th | New London | 3 July |
| Tyler, Elnathan B. | Corporal | 14th | Middletown | 3 July |
| Tyrrell, John M. | Private | 17th | Fairfield | 2 July |
| Upson, William R. | Private | 20th | Southington | 3 July |
| Wallace, William | Private | 17th | Bridgeport | 3 July |
| Ward, Thomas | Sergeant | 27th | New Haven | 2 July |
| Warner, George W. | Private | 20th | Bethany | 3 July |
| Warren, Eugene | Private | 17th | Westport | 1 July |
| Weinberg, Francis | Private | 17th | New Canaan | 1 July |
| Wells, Charles S. | Private | 17th | Huntington | 1 July |
| Whiting, David W. | Corporal | 14th | Vernon | 3 July |
| Whitlock, Nephi | Private | 17th | Ridgefield | 1 July |
| Whitney, Morando H. | Private | 17th | Darien | 2 July |
| Whittlesey, Samuel | Private | 17th | Trumbull | 1 July |
| Williamson, John E. | Private | 27th | New Haven | 2 July |
| Wilmot, Mordaunt L. | Private | 20th | Naugatuck | 3 July |
| Wilson, French | Captain | 17th | Stratford | 1 July |
| Worthington, Thomas E. | Private | 20th | Derby | 2 July |

## Wounded and Captured

| Name | Rank | Regiment | Residence | Date |
|------|------|----------|-----------|------|
| Austen, Jacob | Private | 17th | Ridgefield | 1 July |
| Birdsell, James | Private | 17th | Greenwich | 1 July |
| Colgan, Matthew | Private | 17th | Newtown | 1 July |
| Dudley, Frederick A. | Surgeon | 14th | New Haven | 3 July |
| Hogan, John | Private | 27th | New Haven | 2 July |
| Holley, Albert | Sergeant | 17th | Norwalk | 1 July |
| Kilcullen, Thomas M. | Private | 27th | New Haven | 2 July |
| McNally, Francis | Private | 17th | Norwalk | 1 July |
| Mallett, Charles S. | Private | 17th | Easton | 1 July |
| Northrup, Alpheus | Private | 17th | Newtown | 2 July |
| Norton, Patrick | Private | 17th | New Canaan | 1 July |
| Pattenden, Ebenezer J. | Private | 17th | New Canaan | 1 July |
| Remington, Seth | Private | 17th | New Canaan | 1 July |

## Missing in Action

| Name | Rank | Regiment | Residence | Date |
|------|------|----------|-----------|------|
| Buttery, John D. | Private | 17th | Stamford | 2 July |
| Cable, James W. | Private | 17th | Fairfield | 1 July |
| Cavanagh, John | Private | 17th | Fairfield | 1 July |
| Lavey, James | Private | 17th | Bridgeport | 1 July |
| Nobles, Calvin | Private | 17th | Norwalk | 2 July |
| Stevens, Joseph | Private | 27th | New Haven | 2 July |
| Walsh, John | Private | 17th | Newtown | 2 July |

(No further record on 7 men listed as "missing in action.")

## Captured

| Name | Rank | Regiment | Residence | Date |
|------|------|----------|-----------|------|
| Acker, John | Private | 17th | New Canaan | 1 July |
| Allen, George W. | Private | 17th | Fairfield | 3 July |
| Allen, Theodore | Private | 17th | Westport | 2 July |
| Bachelder, Cyrus T. | Sergeant | 17th | Bridgeport | 1 July |
| Bailey, James H. | Private | 17th | Danbury | 1 July |
| Ball, William C. | Private | 17th | New Canaan | 1 July |
| Barnes, James | Private | 5th | New Haven | 2 July |
| Bartram, David S. | 2d Lieutenant | 17th | Redding | 1 July |
| Batterson, John H. | Private | 17th | Norwalk | 1 July |
| Bennett, Jerome | Private | 17th | Bridgeport | 1 July |
| Bigelow, Henry B. | Private | 17th | Newtown | 2 July |
| Bossa, Norbert | Corporal | 17th | New Canaan | 1 July |
| Bradley, Lewis | Private | 17th | Danbury | 1 July |
| Bronson, Orrin L. | Private | 17th | Danbury | 1 July |
| Brophy, James | Private | 17th | Norwalk | 1 July |
| Brotherton, Charles | Private | 17th | Danbury | 1 July |

## Captured (continued)

| Name | Rank | Regiment | Residence | Date |
|------|------|----------|-----------|------|
| Brush, Theodore | Corporal | 17th | Norwalk | 1 July |
| Buttery, George M. | Corporal | 17th | Wilton | 2 July |
| Cahill, John | Private | 17th | Norwalk | 1 July |
| Chase, Dennis O. | Private | 17th | Westport | 2 July |
| Christison, George B. | Private | 17th | Stamford | 1 July |
| Cooley, Henry M. | Sergeant | 14th | Bridgeport | 2 July |
| Cusher, Joseph | Private | 27th | Branford | 2 July |
| Cutler, Alfred A. | Private | 17th | Norwalk | 1 July |
| Daniels, William L. | Sergeant | 17th | Danbury | 1 July |
| Danneth, Frederick | Sergeant | 5th | Middletown | 2 July |
| Dickens, George | Private | 17th | Danbury | 1 July |
| Donovan, Timothy | Private | 17th | Norwalk | 1 July |
| Downes, William H. | Private | 17th | Norwalk | 1 July |
| Finch, Washington I. | Private | 17th | Greenwich | 1 July |
| French, James W. | Private | 14th | Monroe | 2 July |
| Geathy, John | Private | 14th | Bridgeport | 2 July |
| Gillespie, William | Private | 17th | Stamford | 1 July |
| Gregory, George H. | Private | 17th | Stratford | 1 July |
| Hale, Nathan | Private | 17th | Fairfield | 3 July |
| Harmon, James | Private | 17th | New Fairfield | 1 July |
| Hayes, Dennis | Private | 17th | Newtown | 2 July |
| Hine, Samuel | Private | 27th | New Haven | 2 July |
| Hubbard, Calvin A. | Corporal | 5th | Seymour | 2 July |
| Hubbell, William L. | Captain | 17th | Bridgeport | 1 July |
| Hugh, James | Private | 17th | Weston | 2 July |
| Humphrey, Henry E. | Private | 17th | Norwalk | 2 July |
| Hunt, Daniel | Private | 17th | Bethlehem | 3 July |
| Jacobs, William | Corporal | 14th | Bridgeport | 2 July |
| Jarvis, John J. | Private | 17th | Ridgefield | 2 July |
| Judd, Horace Q. | Corporal | 17th | Ridgefield | 1 July |
| June, John L. | Private | 17th | Stamford | 1 July |
| Kabel, John V. | Private | 17th | Bridgeport | 3 July |
| Lee, William | Private | 27th | New Haven | 2 July |
| Lewis, John F. | Private | 17th | Bridgeport | 1 July |
| Lewis, Luther W. | Private | 17th | Bridgeport | 1 July |
| Lockwood, Joseph H. | Private | 17th | New Canaan | 1 July |
| Lowdon, John A. | Private | 17th | Greenwich | 1 July |
| McConnell, John | Private | 17th | Ridgefield | 1 July |
| Moore, George | Private | 17th | Norwalk | 1 July |
| Morrell, George | Private | 17th | Greenwich | 1 July |
| Morris, Theodore S. | Private | 17th | Danbury | 1 July |
| Northrop, David | Private | 17th | Ridgefield | 1 July |
| Noyes, D. Pardee | 1st Sergeant | 5th | Derby | 2 July |
| Otis, William | Private | 17th | Danbury | 1 July |
| Painter, Jasper E. | Private | 17th | Norwalk | 1 July |

## Captured (continued)

| Name | Rank | Regiment | Residence | Date |
|------|------|----------|-----------|------|
| Palmer, Lewis | Private | 17th | Greenwich | 1 July |
| Palmer, Solomon | Private | 17th | Greenwich | 1 July |
| Peck, Benjamin | Private | 17th | Greenwich | 1 July |
| Perry, James | Corporal | 17th | Westport | 2 July |
| Perry, Roscoe | Corporal | 17th | Westport | 2 July |
| Raymond, Cyrus | Private | 17th | New Canaan | 2 July |
| Robinson, John | Corporal | 5th | Westport | 2 July |
| Rusco, Dewitt C. | Private | 17th | New Canaan | 1 July |
| Saunders, George P. | Private | 17th | Norwalk | 2 July |
| Sclipp, William | Private | 17th | Bridgeport | 1 July |
| Sears, George | Private | 17th | Danbury | 1 July |
| Seeley, Albert D. | Corporal | 17th | Darien | 1 July |
| Seymour, Richard G. | Private | 17th | Wilton | 1 July |
| Shaughness, Lawrence | Private | 17th | Newtown | 2 July |
| Smith, George W. | Private | 17th | Norwalk | 1 July |
| Smith, Nelson | Private | 17th | Westport | 2 July |
| Smith, Samuel T. | Private | 17th | Norwalk | 2 July |
| Smith, William R. | Private | 17th | Monroe | 1 July |
| Squires, Charles A. | Corporal | 5th | Roxbury | 2 July |
| Warner, Henry A. | Corporal | 17th | Bridgeport | 1 July |
| Warren, William H. | Private | 17th | Danbury | 1 July |
| Weed, George W. | Corporal | 17th | New Canaan | 2 July |
| Weed, Levi St. John | Private | 17th | New Canaan | 2 July |
| Welch, Moses C. | Chaplain | 5th | Hartford | 2 July |
| Westerfield, William C. | Private | 17th | Norwalk | 2 July |
| Wheeler, Moses W. | Private | 17th | Danbury | 1 July |
| Whitney, Horace | Sergeant | 17th | Darien | 2 July |
| Wirtz, William | Private | 17th | Bridgeport | 1 July |
| Wood, William L. | Private | 17th | Greenwich | 1 July |
| Woodin, Gilbert | Corporal | 17th | Fairfield | 1 July |

## CONNECTICUT SOLDIERS BURIED AT GETTYSBURG
### National Cemetery

| Name | Location in Connecticut Plot | Regiment |
|------|------------------------------|----------|
| Benson, Frank J. | A-10 | Co. C, 17th |
| Cassidy, James | B-3 | Co. C, 20th |
| Clement, Moses G. | A-4 | Co. G, 14th |
| Confrey, Michael | A-7 | Co. F, 27th |
| Dibble, Alfred H. | B-1 | Co. G, 14th |
| Dickerman, Joel C. | B-4 | Co. I, 20th |
| Dunn, Patrick | C-1 | Co. D, 27th |
| Farr, Edward B. | A-6 | Co. F, 27th |

| *Name* | *Location in Connecticut Plot* | *Regiment* |
|---|---|---|
| Flynn, James | B-7 | Co. E, 17th |
| Hodge, Nelson | B-2 | Co. I, 14th |
| Marsh, William D. | A-3 | Co.G,14th |
| Metcalf, John W. | B-9 | Co. F, 17th |
| Mulvey, Bernard | A-9 | Co. I, 20th |
| Perry, John D. | A-8 | Co. F, 20th |
| Puffer, Joseph | A-2 | Co. I, 14th |
| Purdy, Daniel | B-6 | Co.C,17th |
| Roberts, Charles H. | B-5 | Co. F, 20th |
| Whitlock, Joseph S. | A-11 | Co.C,17th |
| Wilson, William E. | A-1 | Co.D,27th |

## Evergreen Cemetery (Civil War Section)

| *Name* | *Regiment* |
|---|---|
| Clark, Aaron A. | Co.G,14th |
| Wilcox, Alva E. | Co.D,17th |

There are two more men from the state buried in Evergreen who did not fight in the battle: Charles S. Pease and William R. Palmer. Pease, a native of Glastenbury, was serving with Company M of the 1st Connecticut Cavalry when it traveled to Gettysburg in July 1865 to be part of the ceremonies to dedicate the cornerstone of the Soldier's National Monument in the cemetery. According to the *Gettysburg Compiler,* 17 July 1865, Pease was just 15 when "he died in camp." He was "a special favorite in his company, and his death was greatly lamented by his comrades, who had him interred in Ever Green Cemetery, and left orders for the erection of a fine tombstone over his grave." William R. Palmer, a native of Bridgeport, served with Captain Sterling's 2d Connecticut Light Artillery during its entire term of service and was mustered out in August 1865.

## CONNECTICUT CASUALTIES SERVING WITH OTHER UNITS AT GETTYSBURG
### Killed or Mortally Wounded

| *Name* | *Rank* | *Regiment* | *Connecticut Residence* | *Date* |
|---|---|---|---|---|
| Barri, Thomas O. | Captain | 11th U.S. Infantry | Not stated | 2 July |
| Burke, John | Corporal | 14th U.S. Infantry | Hartford | 2 July |
| Gans, Frederick W. | Private | 17th U.S. Infantry | Hartford | 2 July |

### Killed or Mortally Wounded (continued)

| Name | Rank | Regiment | Connecticut Residence | Date |
|------|------|----------|----------------------|------|
| Murray, Thomas | Private | 14th U.S. Infantry | New Haven | 1 July |
| Stevens, Edsen | Private | 14th U.S. Infantry | New London | 3 July |

### Wounded

| Name | Rank | Regiment | Connecticut Residence | Date |
|------|------|----------|----------------------|------|
| Crawford, Richard | Lieutenant | 7th U.S. Infantry | Bridgeport | 2 July |
| Dudley, W. W. | Lt. Colonel | 19th Indiana | New Haven | 1 July |
| Eagin, James | Private | 14th U.S. Infantry | Hartford | 2 July |
| Gaylord, Ransom | Lieutenant | 70th New York | Colchester | 2 July |
| Miller, Charles W. | Private | 14th U.S. Infantry | West Haven | 3 July |
| Porter, Isaac | Lieutenant | 68th Pennsylvania | New Britain | 2 July |
| Stannis, John A. | Lieutenant | 14th Indiana | Hartford | 3 July |

### Captured

| Name | Rank | Regiment | Connecticut Residence | Date |
|------|------|----------|----------------------|------|
| McCarrick, Robert | Private | 20th New York | Lakeville | 1 July |

# NOTES

## I CONNECTICUT ON THE MARCH: THE ROADS TO GETTYSBURG

1. William T. Lusk, *War Letters of William Thompson Lusk*, 284–85.

2. Lusk, 275. Born in Norwich in 1838, Lusk attended Yale and studied medicine in Germany before the war. He refused an offer to serve on the staff of Governor William Buckingham, enlisting instead as a private in the 79th New York Volunteers and distinguishing himself in a number of battles. After the war he had a successful medical practice. See Lusk, 14ff.

3. Total Connecticut casualties compiled from *Record of Service of Connecticut Men in the Army and Navy of the United States during the War of the Rebellion* (hereafter cited as *Record of Service*); the statistics on Connecticut's manpower and total enlistments are found in John Niven, *Connecticut for the Union: The Role of the State in the Civil War*, 87.

4. Henry F. Prindle to Parents, Letter, 22 June 1863, Private Collection of Robert Angelovich, Torrington, Connecticut.

5. For a discussion of Lee's strategy, see John S. Mosby, "The Confederate Cavalry in the Gettysburg Campaign" in *Battles and Leaders of the Civil War* 3:252ff. See also James Longstreet, "Lee's Invasion of Pennsylvania" in *Battles and Leaders* 3:249–50.

6. Longstreet, "Lee's Invasion of Pennsylvania" in *Battles and Leaders* 3:249.

7. Cited in Freeman Cleaves, *Meade of Gettysburg*, 131.

8. William H. Warren, Diary, Sterling Library, Yale University, New Haven.

9. *Record of Service*, 341. Starting in 1850, William Noble and Phineas T. Barnum began purchasing large tracts of land in East Bridgeport in the hopes of developing an industrial community. Their subsequent success in bringing firms like Winchester Arms, Union Metallic Cartridge Company, and Bridgeport Brass to the area resulted in enormous profits for both men. See Niven, 334–35.

10. Edward E. Marvin, *The Fifth Regiment, Connecticut Volunteers*, 245.

11. John W. Storrs, *The Twentieth Connecticut, A Regimental History*, 57.

12. Charles D. Page, *History of the Fourteenth Connecticut Volunteer Infantry*, 119.

13. *Record of Service*, 825–26.

14. For the story of the knapsack burning, see Jerome B. Lucke, *History of the New Haven Grays*, 287. The summary of the regimental record is found in *Record of Service*, 827.

15. See William A. Croffut and John M. Morris, *The Military and Civil History of Connecticut during the War of 1861–65*, 236.

16. Statistics relating to regimental strengths and casualties were taken from *Record of Service* and from Croffut and Morris.

17. Patricia L. Faust, ed., *Historical Times Illustrated Encyclopedia of the Civil War*, 671, 844. See also *Dedication of the Equestrian Statue of Major-General John Sedgwick Erected on the Battlefield of Gettysburg by the State of Connecticut, June 19, 1913*, 31ff.

18. Faust, ed., 792.

19. E. P. Leddy and E. J. Lonergan, *The Connecticut Civil War Centennial: Connecticut Military and Naval Leaders of the Civil War*, 22ff.

## 2 "ALWAYS BRAVE AND ENERGETIC":
### THE 17TH CONNECTICUT AT BARLOW'S KNOLL

1. "Letter from Major-General Henry Heth, of A. P. Hill's Corps, A. N. V," *Southern Historical Society Papers* 4 (Oct. 1877): 157.

2. *The War of the Rebellion: A Compilation of the Official Records of the Union and Confederate Armies* ser. 1, vol. 43:927 (hereafter cited as *OR*).

3. Henry J. Hunt, "First Day" in *Battles and Leaders* 3:274.

4. See Benjamin F. Charles, "Hooker's Appointment and Removal" in *Battles and Leaders* 3:240.

5. Stephen Minot Weld, *War Diary and Letters of Stephen Minot Weld, 1861–1865*, 230.

6. Abner Doubleday, *Chancellorsville and Gettysburg*, 131.

7. Ibid., 134.

8. *OR*, 27 (subsequent references to vol. 27 unless otherwise noted), 1:702; Charles C. Coffin, *Four Years of Fighting*, 296; Warren, Diary, 84.

9. Coffin, 270.

10. *OR* 1:702.

11. Oliver Otis Howard, *Autobiography of Oliver Otis Howard* 1:413–14.

12. Ibid., 408–9, 414.

13. *OR* 1:721; Warren W. Hassler, *Crisis at the Crossroads: The First Day at Gettysburg*, 149–50.

14. *OR* 1:704.

15. Carl Schurz, *The Autobiography of Carl Schurz*, 257.

16. *OR* 1:702.

17. Schurz, 259.

18. Warren, Diary, 84.

19. See Doty letter in William H. Warren, "Seventeenth Connecticut: The Record of a Yankee Regiment in the War for the Union," Scrapbooks, Sterling

Library, Yale University, New Haven. This letter was quoted at length in a newspaper article submitted to the *Danbury News* as part of a series Warren published as the first effort toward compiling a regimental history. Warren, a native of Danbury and a member of Company C, devoted much of his life to collecting letters, photographs, and other memorabilia from his regimental comrades, apparently hoping to publish the official regimental history. He never completed the task, but just before his death deposited eight large, bound typescript volumes at the Bridgeport Public Library, a collection which he noted was his eighth revision.

20. War Department tablet marking Battery G, 4th U.S. Artillery (Wilkeson) at Barlow's Knoll, Gettysburg National Military Park. For a very useful compendium of all the monument and tablet inscriptions at Gettysburg, see Roy E. Frampton, *One Country, One Flag: The Strife of Brothers Is Past.*

21. *OR,* vol. 44:492.

22. C. Frederick Betts of Company F to Henry Allen as quoted in William H. Warren Scrapbooks, Bridgeport Public Library, Bridgeport.

23. Croffut and Morris, 85; *OR* 1:717.

24. *OR* 1:717. At the time of the battle, Josiah Benner lived on the farm with his wife, Edith, and eight children. His property included a substantial two-story brick house, stone barn, several outbuildings, and 146 acres—all valued at $11,400 in 1860. According to stories passed down by Josiah's daughters Anne and Hattie, the family remained on the property until ordered to leave by the Confederates that afternoon. For this information I am indebted to Mr. William E. Jordan, current owner of the Benner house. See also Josiah Benner file, Gettysburg National Military Park, and the very helpful genealogical study of the Benner family by Steward Herman, *Daniel's Line,* 135–37.

25. *OR* 1:717. The text of a photograph of the house in the possession of Mr. Benner's great-grandson asserts that "the house was struck by eight shells, one passing through, setting fire to the building; but for the continuing efforts of Mr. Benner the house would have been burnt." This information is courtesy of Mr. William E. Jordan.

26. Doubleday, 142; Howard, 416.

27. Hunt, "First Day" in *Battles and Leaders* 3:281.

28. John B. Gordon, *Reminiscences of the Civil War,* 150–51.

29. *OR* 1:712. See also Warren, Diary, 84.

30. Croffut and Morris, 391.

31. Doty as cited in Warren Scrapbooks; William F. Fox, *New York at Gettysburg* 1:20; Warren, Diary, 87; *OR* 1:717. Pvt. J. Henry Blakeman of Company D, 17th Connecticut, noted in a letter to his mother on 4 July, "I can hardly bring my mind to tell you that Stephen [Stephen Crofut, Company D] was killed by the same volly [sic] that wounded me. He was within three feet of me was shot through the head and killed instantly. Stephen was liked by the whole Co. and will be much mourned. I know it will almost kill his mother but reality is better than suspense and what I tell you you can depend on." See J. Henry Blakeman, Letter, Book 40, Lewis Leigh Collection, U.S. Army Military History Institute, Carlisle Barracks, Carlisle, Pa.

32. Gordon, 151.

33. Fox 1:20; Betts as cited in Warren Scrapbooks. The body of Lieutenant Colonel Fowler was never recovered. Lieutenant Doty noted that members of the unit returned to Barlow's Knoll and 4 July in an effort to recover those buried there but found that Fowler and many others had been "stripped of all but underclothing by the rebels and thrown into a ditch, ten or twelve at a time and covered over . . . so it was impossible to recognize them." See Doty letter in Warren Scrapbooks. In 1889 the veterans of the 17th erected a flag-pole on Barlow's Knoll to mark the spot where Fowler was killed.

34. Warren, Diary, 87.

35. OR 1:717.

36. Ibid. 2:479; 1:717.

37. Hunt, "First Day" in Battles and Leaders 3:281–82.

38. John Vautier, History of the 88th Pennsylvania Regiment, 149.

39. OR 1:717.

40. Fox 1:22.

41. Hassler, 130.

42. Howard 1:419; OR 1:718.

43. E. P. Halstead, "Incidents of the First Day at Gettysburg" in Battles and Leaders 3:285.

44. Hunt, "First Day" in ibid. 3:283; Hassler, 140.

45. Record of Service, 34.

46. The Silliman letter appears in Edward Marcus, ed., A New Canaan Private in the Civil War: Letters of Justus M. Silliman, 17th Connecticut Volunteers, 41.


3 "MY POOR REGIMENT":
THE 27TH CONNECTICUT AND THE WHEAT FIELD FIGHT


1. Frank L. Byrne and Andrew T. Weaver, eds., Haskell of Gettysburg: His Life and Civil War Papers, 120; "A Letter from General Meade" in Battles and Leaders 2:414.

2. "From General Hancock's Official Report" in ibid. 3:287; Edwin B. Coddington, The Gettysburg Campaign: A Study in Command, 204.

3. Page, 138.

4. OR 1:705.

5. Page, 138.

6. Byrne and Weaver, eds., Haskell, 106; "The Opposing Forces at Gettysburg, Pa.: The Union Army" in Battles and Leaders 3:434.

7. Byrne and Weaver, eds., Haskell, 112.

8. Henry J. Hunt, "The Second Day at Gettysburg" in Battles and Leaders 3:296.

9. Ibid.; Leddy and Lonergan, 27.

10. Coddington, 726.

11. See James Longstreet, "Lee's Right Wing at Gettysburg" in Battles and Leaders 3:339–43.

12. Ibid. 3:341.

13. See J. B. Kershaw, "Kershaw's Brigade at Gettysburg" in *Battles and Leaders* 3:331–32.

14. William Swinton, *Campaigns of the Army of the Potomac*, 344.

15. Joseph H. Twichell to sister, Letter, 5 July 1863, Beinecke Rare Book and Manuscript Library, Yale University, New Haven.

16. Ibid.

17. Swinton, 347.

18. See H. S. Melcher, "The 20th Maine at Little Round Top" in *Battles and Leaders* 3:314–15.

19. Ibid.; see also Hunt, "Second Day" in ibid. 3:311.

20. *OR* 2:369.

21. *Record of Service*, 827.

22. Hunt, "Second Day" in *Battles and Leaders* 3:299.

23. Byrne and Weaver, eds., *Haskell*, 117–18.

24. *OR* 1:379.

25. Ibid.

26. Ibid., 400.

27. Ibid. 2:368.

28. Winthrop D. Sheldon, *The Twenty-Seventh, A Regimental History*, 91. See also Lucke, 294–95.

29. Sheldon, 91. Near the road that skirts the northern edge of the Wheatfield lies a small stone marker that reads: "In memory of Lt. Col. Henry C. Merwin who fell mortally wounded where the monument of his Regiment stands."

30. John Page Nicholson, ed., *Pennsylvania at Gettysburg* 2:701.

31. Sheldon, 77. Chapman, also a former member of the New Haven Grays, was one of the first recruits of the 27th Connecticut, which he helped to raise, serving as lieutenant of Company H. He distinguished himself at Fredericksburg and was promoted to captain just before Gettysburg. In the words of Jerome Lucke, "he was conspicuous for his worth and merits, a sincere patriot, a loving son, and beloved by his companions in arms" (296). A small tablet at the southwest corner of the Wheatfield notes: "Here fell Jed. Chapman, Capt. Co. H. 27th Conn. Vols."

32. Sheldon, 77.

33. Monuments along what is now called Brooke Avenue designate the forward position gained by the 2d Delaware on the left and, progressively to its right, the 64th New York, 53d Pennsylvania, 27th Connecticut, and 145th Pennsylvania. Chiseled on the front of the 27th Connecticut monument are the words: "Advanced position of this Regiment in the Brigade Charge July 2, 1863." A few feet to the right and just below the top of the ridge is a small tablet also noting where the regiment planted its colors.

34. Undated letter of Almond E. Clark, Company C, 27th Connecticut, Connecticut Historical Society, Hartford. See also Almond E. Clark, "The 27th Connecticut at Gettysburg," *National Tribune*, 10 Oct. 1918.

35. Sheldon, 77; *OR* 1:401.

36. *OR* 1:401; Clark, "27th Connecticut," *National Tribune*.

37. Sheldon, 79.

38. Ibid., 80.

4 "WE HAD A HAND-TO-HAND CONFLICT":
THE 17TH CONNECTICUT AT EAST CEMETERY HILL

1. *OR* 1:718; Edward N. Whittier, "The Left Attack (Ewell's) at Gettysburg" in *Civil War Papers, Military Order of the Loyal Legion of the United States* 1:85.
2. *OR* 1:718.
3. Ibid.
4. Statistics compiled from *Record of Service*, 643ff; *OR* 1:718.
5. Whittier in *Civil War Papers* 1:84–85.
6. *OR* 1:715.
7. Gordon, 154.
8. Whittier in *Civil War Papers* 1:84–85.
9. Ibid., 86.
10. Coddington, 430.
11. *OR* 2:480.
12. Ibid. 2:718; Whittier in *Civil War Papers* 1:87.
13. Daniels cited in Warren Scrapbooks.
14. Whittier in *Civil War Papers* 1:88.
15. *OR* 1:718.
16. Daniels cited in Warren Scrapbooks.
17. Whittier in *Civil War Papers* 1:90.
18. *OR* 2:480.
19. Ibid. 1:718.
20. Walter Clark, *Histories of the Several Regiments and Battalions from North Carolina in the Great War 1861–1865* 1:316–17; Fox 2:404.
21. Whittier in *Civil War Papers* 1:90.
22. *OR* 1:718; Clark 2:137.
23. *OR* 2:486; Whittier in *Civil War Papers* 1:91.
24. Swinton, 354. See also *OR* 2:480–81.
25. *OR* 2:481.
26. Ibid.
27. Ibid. 1:718; Clark 2:137.
28. Coddington, 437; Charles S. Wainwright, *A Diary of Battle*, 246; *OR* 1:718.
29. Edward Porter Alexander, *Military Memoirs of a Confederate*, 443; *Record of Service*, 643ff.
30. *Record of Service*, 34. A few months after Gettysburg, Major Brady left the service, discharged for disability. On 23 November 1863 he joined the Twentieth Regiment, Veterans Reserve Corps, where he was later breveted lieutenant colonel and then colonel. He was honorably discharged on 15 December 1866, and after the war he engaged in business in Torrington, Connecticut, and later in Fayetteville, North Carolina. He died in Fayetteville in 1905. See Warren Scrapbooks 5:182ff. Bordering the lane called Wainwright Avenue and directly below the Evergreen Cemetery entrance and the gun emplacements of Captain Weidrich's artillerymen, there stands a granite shaft honoring the 17th Connecticut. The text on it reads: "The regiment

formed in the line of battle on East Cemetery Hill, and on the evening of July 2nd took position here and was engaged in repulsing the desperate night assault of Hays' and Hoke's Brigades."

## 5 "ONLY A BATTLE WOULD GIVE US POSSESSION": THE 5TH AND 20TH CONNECTICUT AT CULP'S HILL

1. *OR* 2:319.

2. Leddy and Lonergan, 29.

3. *OR* 1:705; Francis A. Walker, "Meade at Gettysburg" in *Battles and Leaders* 3:409.

4. *OR* 1:788.

5. Ibid.

6. Storrs, 218.

7. *OR* 1:790.

8. Coddington, 342.

9. Ibid.; Jesse H. Jones, "The Breastworks at Cult's Hill" in *Battles and Leaders* 3:316.

10. Storrs, 82–83.

11. Ibid., 264–65.

12. Ibid., 86; George Sears Greene, "The Breastworks at Culp's Hill" in *Battles and Leaders* 3:317.

13. Abner C. Smith to wife, Letter, 4 July 1863, Connecticut State Library, Hartford.

14. *OR* 1:380, 793.

15. Storrs, 87–88.

16. Green in *Battles and Leaders* 3:317.

17. Ibid.

18. Jones in ibid. 3:316; Greene in ibid. 3:316.

19. Greene in ibid. 3:317.

20. Marvin, 280.

21. Ibid., 275; *Record of Service*, 224.

22. Coddington, 467.

23. Storrs, 92; *OR* 1:793.

24. *OR* 1:791.

25. Shelby Foote, *The Civil War* 2:526–27.

26. *OR* 1:775; Storrs, 194.

27. *OR* 1:784.

28. Ibid., 779.

29. Ibid., 775, 793.

30. Henry J. Hunt, "The Third Day at Gettysburg" in *Battles and Leaders* 3:369.

31. *OR* 1:784.

32. Ibid., 793.

33. Storrs, 107. Warner survived his wounds and was discharged in October 1863. He returned to his hometown of Bethany, where he became a suc-

cessful businessman and raised a family. He returned to the battlefield with other veterans of the 20th Connecticut to attend the dedication of the unit monument on Culp's Hill on 3 July 1885, and his comrades honored him by asking that he unveil the new monument. According to the *Gettysburg Compiler,* 7 July 1885, "the cord attached to the flag was tied around his body, and taking a few steps back the beautiful sarcophagus was displayed."

34. Storrs, 93; Coddington, 188.

35. Greene in *Battles and Leaders* 3:317; *OR* 1:682–83.

36. *OR* 1:784; Smith, Letter; Greene in *Battles and Leaders* 3:317.

37. *OR* 1:791; Marvin, 275.

38. *OR* 1:785; Information based on inscription on 20th Connecticut monument, Culp's Hill; Storrs, 95–96.

39. Coddington, 496; Smith, Letter.

40. Storrs, 99–100.

41. *OR* 1:791.


6 "THE LAST THROW OF THE DICE":
THE 14TH CONNECTICUT AND THE FIGHT FOR CEMETERY RIDGE

1. Lusk, 247–48.

2. Longstreet, "Lee's Right Wing" in *Battles and Leaders* 3:343.

3. John Gibbon, "The Council of War on the Second Day" in ibid. 3:314.

4. Hunt, "Second Day" in ibid. 3:296; Page, 139.

5. Henry S. Stevens, *Souvenir of the Excursion to Battlefields by the Society of the Fourteenth Connecticut Regiment and Reunion at Antietam, September 1891,* 12.

6. Page, 140–41.

7. Swinton, 351; Stevens, 15; *OR* 1:453, 467.

8. *Minutes of the 19th Annual Meeting of "The Society of the Fourteenth Connecticut,"* 7.

9. Stevens, 15; *OR* 1:437; Page, 142.

10. Page, 143.

11. *OR* 2:359.

12. Stevens, 16.

13. For much of this information I am indebted to Mr. Elwood Christ of Gettysburg, author of *On a Wide, Hot, Crimson Plain: The Bliss Farm Fight at Gettysburg.* See also Stevens, 16; and *OR* 1:465.

14. Stevens, 20.

15. Page, 145.

16. Stevens, 21.

17. Ibid.

18. Ibid., 20–21.

19. *OR* 1:467.

20. Alexander, 420.

21. Byrne and Weaver, eds., *Haskell,* 155–56; Page, 149.

22. Page, 149.

23. Fairfax Downey, *The Guns of Gettysburg*, 205.

24. Nicholson, ed. 2:626.

25. *Record of Service*, 105.

26. Hunt, "Third Day" in *Battles and Leaders* 3:374.

27. Edward Porter Alexander, "The Great Charge and Artillery Fighting at Gettysburg" in ibid. 3:362–63.

28. *OR* 1:480, 467; Page, 151.

29. *OR* 2:359.

30. Page, 151.

31. Nicholson, ed. 2:630.

32. *OR* 2:386.

33. Ibid. 1:349–50.

34. Page, 152.

35. Hunt, "Third Day" in *Battles and Leaders* 3:375.

36. Page, 155.

37. Clark 5:156–57; *OR* 1:428–29.

38. Clark 3:238.

39. *OR* 2:1000.

40. Ibid. 1:428–29.

41. Clark 2:692–93.

42. Ibid. 5:110; Page, 153; Stevens, 31.

43. Clark 5:110–11. See also *OR* 1:356; 2:666–67.

44. Stevens, 32; Page, 155–56.

45. Alexander McNeil to David G. Porter, "Bristowsburg, Virginia," Letter, 16 August 1863, Connecticut Historical Society, Hartford. McNeil was captured in early 1864 and died at Salisbury Prison in North Carolina later that year.

46. *OR* 1:467–68.

47. Ibid., 349–50; 2:265.

48. *Record of Service*, 105.

49. George T. Fleming, *Life and Letters of General Alexander Hays*, 464–65; Byrne and Weaver, eds., *Haskell*, 174; A. L. Long and Marcus J. Wright, eds., *Memoirs of Robert E. Lee*, 296.

50. Stevens, 31.

51. Pierce fought with the regiment throughout the war, and he was promoted to corporal in November 1863. Honorably discharged in May 1865, he returned to Meriden where he learned engraving and worked at the Meriden Silver Company. He died in 1916, survived by a wife and two sons.

52. Loren H. Goodrich to unknown recipient, Letter, 17 July 1863, Connecticut Historical Society, Hartford.

7 "THEY FELT THE SHOCK OF BATTLE": THE AFTERMATH

1. Gordon, 163–64.

2. *Gettysburg Compiler*, 22 Sept. 1896.

3. *OR* 1:781–82.

4. Ibid., 789.

5. Harlan P. Ruggs, Diary, 4 June 1861–15 June 1865, pp. 60–61, Connecticut Historical Society, Hartford; Stevens, 32.

6. *Record of Service*, 551.

7. Ibid., 691.

8. Ibid., 641–42.

9. Ibid., 828.

10. Ibid., 106.

11. The first regimental monument was erected by the 2d Massachusetts Regiment in Spangler's Meadow in 1879, and only those monuments to the 91st and 88th Pennsylvania preceded a group including the 14th and 17th Connecticut erected in the summer of 1884. See John M. Vanderslice, *Gettysburg, Then and Now*, 364ff.

12. Julius W. Knowlton and Henry S. Stevens, *Address Delivered at the Dedication of the Monument of the 14th Connecticut Volunteers at Gettysburg, Pa., July 3rd, 1884*, 25.

13. Minutes of the Business Meetings of the 5th Connecticut Volunteer Association, 8 August 1910–31 August, 1920, Manuscript, pp. 17–19 (8–9 August 1910), George McNamara Collection, Philadelphia.

14. *Dedication of the Equestrian Statue of Major-General John Sedgwick*, 72.

# BIBLIOGRAPHY

## MANUSCRIPTS

Benner, Josiah. Vertical File, Gettysburg National Military Park, Gettysburg, Pennsylvania.

Blakeman, J. Henry. Letter, 4 July 1863. Lewis Leigh Collection, United States Army Military History Institute, Carlisle Barracks, Carlisle, Pa.

Clark, Almond E. Undated Letter (ca. July 1863). Connecticut Historical Society, Hartford.

Goodrich, Loren H. Letter, 17 July 1863. Connecticut Historical Society, Hartford.

McNeil, Alexander. Letter, 16 August 1863. Connecticut Historical Society, Hartford.

Minutes of the Business Meetings of the 5th Connecticut Volunteers Association, 8 August 1910–31 August 1920. Manuscript. Private Collection of George McNamara, Philadelphia.

Prindle, Henry F. Letter, 22 June 1863. Private Collection of Robert Angelovich, Torrington, Connecticut.

Ruggs, Harlan P. Diary, 4 June 1861–15 June 1865. Connecticut Historical Society, Hartford.

Smith, Abner C. Letter, 4 July 1863. Connecticut State Library, Hartford.

Twichell, Joseph H. Letter, 5 July 1863. Beinecke Rare Book and Manuscript Library, Yale University, New Haven.

Warren, William H. Diary and Scrapbooks. Sterling Library, Yale University, New Haven.

Warren, William H. Scrapbooks. Bridgeport Public Library, Bridgeport.

## NEWSPAPERS AND JOURNALS

*Gettysburg Compiler* 1884, 1896
*National Tribune* 1918

## PUBLISHED SOURCES

Alexander, Edward Porter. *Military Memoirs of a Confederate*. New York: Charles Scribner's Sons, 1907.

*Battles and Leaders of the Civil War.* 4 vols. New York: Century Company, 1884.

Benet, Stephen Vincent. *John Brown's Body*. New York: Holt, Rinehart and Winston, 1968.

Busey, John W. *These Honored Dead: The Union Casualties at Gettysburg.* Hightstown, N.J.: Longstreet House, 1988.

Busey, John W., and David G. Martin. *Regimental Strengths at Gettysburg.* Baltimore: Gateway Press, 1982.

Byrne, Frank L., and Andrew T. Weaver, eds. *Haskell of Gettysburg: His Life and Civil War Papers.* Kent, Ohio: Kent State Univ. Press, 1989.

Christ, Elwood W. *Across a Wide, Hot, Crimson Plain: The Bliss Farm Fight at Gettysburg.* Baltimore: Butternut and Blue, 1993.

*Civil War Papers, Military Order of the Loyal Legion of the United States (MOLLUS).* Vol. 1. Boston, 1900.

Clark, Walter. *Histories of the Several Regiments and Battalions from North Carolina in the Great War 1861–1865.* 5 vols. Goldsboro, N.C.: Nash Brothers, 1901.

Cleaves, Freeman. *Meade of Gettysburg.* Norman, Okla.: Univ. of Oklahoma Press, 1960.

Coddington, Edwin B. *The Gettysburg Campaign: A Study in Command.* New York: Charles Scribner's Sons, 1968.

Coffin, Charles C. *Four Years of Fighting.* Boston: Ticknor and Fields, 1866.

Croffut, William A., and John M. Morris. *The Military and Civil History of Connecticut during the War of 1861–65.* New York: Ledyard Bill, 1868.

*Dedication of the Equestrian Statue of Major-General John Sedgwick Erected on the Battlefield of Gettysburg by the State of Connecticut June 19, 1913.* Hartford: State of Connecticut, 1913.

Doubleday, Abner. *Chancellorsville and Gettysburg.* New York: Charles Scribner's, 1882.

Downey, Fairfax. *The Guns of Gettysburg.* New York: David McKay, 1958.

Faust, Patricia L., ed. *Historical Times Illustrated Encyclopedia of the Civil War.* New York: Harper and Row, 1986.

Fleming, George T. *Life and Letters of General Alexander Hays.* Pittsburgh: N.p., 1919.

Foote, Shelby. *The Civil War.* 3 vols. New York: Random House, 1963.

Fox, William F. *New York at Gettysburg.* 3 vols. Albany: J. B. Lyon Company, 1900.

Frampton, Roy E. *One Country, One Flag: The Strife of Brothers Is Past.* 2 vols. Gettysburg, Pa.: Privately published, 1987.

Gordon, John B. *Reminiscences of the Civil War.* New York: Charles Scribner's Sons, 1903.

Hassler, Warren W. *Crisis at the Crossroads: The First Day at Gettysburg.* Tuscaloosa: Univ. of Alabama Press, 1970.

Herman, Stewart. *Daniel's Line.* Shelter Island Heights, N.Y.: Privately published, 1978.

Howard, Oliver Otis. *Autobiography of Oliver Otis Howard.* 2 vols. New York: Baker and Taylor, 1908.

Knowlton, Julius W., and Henry S. Stevens. *Address Delivered at the Dedication of the Monument of the 14th Connecticut Volunteers at Gettysburg, Pa., July 3rd, 1884.* Middletown, Conn.: Pelton and King, 1884.

Krick, Robert K. *The Gettysburg Death Roster: The Confederate Dead at Gettysburg.* 2d ed. Dayton, Ohio: Morningside Bookshop, 1985.

Leedy, E. P., and E. J. Lonergan. *The Connecticut Civil War Centennial: Connecticut Military and Naval Leaders of the Civil War.* Hartford: Civil War Centennial Commission, 1961.

Long, A. L., and Marcus J. Wright, eds. *Memoirs of Robert E. Lee.* Secaucus, N.J.: Blue and Gray Press, 1983.

Lucke, Jerome B. *History of the New Haven Grays.* New Haven: Tuttle, Morehouse and Taylor, 1876.

Lusk, William T. *War Letters of William Thompson Lusk.* New York: Privately published, 1911.

Marcus, Edward, ed. *A New Canaan Private in the Civil War: Letters of Justus M. Silliman, 17th Connecticut Volunteers.* New Canaan, Conn.: New Canaan Historical Society, 1984.

Marvin, Edward E. *The Fifth Regiment, Connecticut Volunteers.* Hartford: Wiley, Waterman and Eaton, 1889.

*Minutes of the 19th Annual Meeting of "The Society of the Fourteenth Connecticut."* Bridgeport, Conn., 1883.

Nicholson, John Page, ed. *Pennsylvania at Gettysburg.* 2 vols. Harrisburg: William Stanley Ray, 1904.

Niven, John. *Connecticut for the Union: The Role of the State in the Civil War.* New Haven: Yale Univ. Press, 1965.

Page, Charles D. *History of the Fourteenth Connecticut Volunteer Infantry.* Meriden, Conn.: Horton Printing Company, 1906.

*Record of Service of Connecticut Men in the Army and Navy of the United States during the War of the Rebellion.* Hartford: Case, Lockwood, and Brainard Company, 1889.

Schurz, Carl. *The Autobiography of Carl Schurz.* New York: Charles Scribner's Sons, 1961.

Sheldon, Winthrop D. *The Twenty-Seventh, A Regimental History.* New Haven: Morris and Benham, 1866.

*Southern Historical Society Papers.* 52 vols. Richmond, Va.: 1876–1939.

Stevens, Henry S. *Souvenir of the Excursion to Battlefields by the Society of the Fourteenth Connecticut Regiment and Reunion at Antietam, September 1891.* Washington, D.C.: Gibson Brothers, 1893.

Storrs, John W. *The Twentieth Connecticut, A Regimental History.* Ansonia, Conn.: Press of the Naugatuck Valley Sentinel, 1886.

Swinton, William. *Campaigns of the Army of the Potomac.* New York: Charles B. Richardson, 1866.

Vanderslice, John M. *Gettysburg, Then and Now.* New York: G. W. Dillingham, 1899.

Vautier, John. *History of the 88th Pennsylvania Regiment.* Philadelphia: J. B. Lippincott, 1894.

Wainwright, Charles S. *A Diary of Battle.* New York: Harcourt, Brace and World, 1962.

Walker, Francis A. *History of the Second Army Corps.* New York: Charles Scribner's Sons, 1886.

*The War of the Rebellion: A Compilation of the Official Records of the Union and Confederate Armies.* 128 vols. Washington, D.C.: Government Printing Office, 1880–1901.

Weld, Stephen Minot. *War Diary and Letters of Stephen Minot Weld, 1861–1865.* Cambridge, Mass.: Riverside Press, 1912.

Whitman, Walt. *Complete Poetry and Collected Prose.* New York: Library of America, 1982.

# INDEX

*Connecticut Yankees at Gettysburg*

was composed in 10/12 Trump Medieval
on a Xyvision system with Linotronic output
by BookMasters, Inc.;
with display type set in Birch
on a Gateway 2000 PC with PageMaker 4.0 and 800 dpi laser output
at Kent State University Press;
printed by sheet-fed offset on 60-pound Glatfelter Natural acid-free stock
with halftones printed in signatures on 70-pound enamel stock,
Smyth sewn and bound over binder's boards
and wrapped with dustjackets printed in two colors
on 80-pound enamel stock and film laminated;
also notch bound with paper covers printed in two colors
on 12-point C1S stock and film laminated
by Braun-Brumfield, Inc.;
designed by Will Underwood;
and published by

*The Kent State University Press*
KENT, OHIO 44242